THE PLACE-NAMES OF EASTERN GWENT

by GRAHAM OSBORNE
& GRAHAM HOBBS

Old Bakehouse Publications

Abertillery

First published in June 1998

ISBN 1 874538 91 3

Published in the U.K. by
Old Bakehouse Publications
Church Street,
Abertillery, Gwent NP3 1EA
Telephone: 01495 212600   Fax: 0195 216222

Made and printed in the U.K.
by J.R. Davies (Printers) Ltd.

Introduction

This book is a companion volume to 'The Place-Names of Western Gwent' which appeared in 1991 and in which the origins of the names of places lying between the rivers Rhymni and Usk were considered. In the present volume the study has been extended to cover the rest of Gwent, i.e. to those places between the rivers Usk and Wye.

Previously, literature on the topic of the place-names of Gwent has been very limited. Interpretations of the major names have appeared, i.e. in 'Enwau Lleoedd' by Sir Ifor Williams (1945 and 1962) and, particularly, in 'The Names of Towns and Cities in Britain' by N. Gelling, W. A. F. Nicolaisen and H. Richards (published in 1970). More recently, some of this ground has been covered in the 'Dictionary of Place-Names of the British Isles' by Adrian Room (published in 1988). But this leaves most of the county uncovered. It is true that Bradney in his 'History of Monmouthshire' proposed meanings for a number of place-names as, indeed did (the late) Canon E. T. Davies in his little booklet of 1972. But much of this work now needs amendment. However, a number of the non-Welsh place-names of Gwent are included in B. G. Charles 'Non-Celtic Place-Names of Wales' (1937).

In 1924 C. J. Evans (writing as 'Shon') compiled quite a comprehensive list of the place-names of Gwent and their meanings in an unpublished dissertation submitted to the National Eisteddfod at Pontypool. Photostat copies of the handwritten work are available at Gwent County Records Office and Newport Library. But this work now requires very considerable revision.

The Book of Llandaff which is the mainly 12th century cartulary (or book of records) of Llandaff Cathedral is a valuable source of early name-forms, particularly for places in Eastern Gwent, especially those sections in which grants of land are recorded (i.e. the 'Llandaff Charters'). The name-forms used in this work are those given in 'The Book of Llan-Dâf' by J. G. Evans, published in 1893, though some of the dates have been taken from Professor Wendy Davies' 'An Early Welsh Microcosm; Studies in the Llandaff Charters' published in 1978.

The procedure adopted in the 'Place-Names of Western Gwent' is employed again in the present work which is also intended to be a compact handbook for the general reader. Attempts have been made to discover early name-forms and these, with later forms, are listed and interpreted. It has again been found to be impractical to present all of the name-forms collected in a book of this size.

Acknowledgement

The authors wish to express their gratitude to members of staff of the Gwent Records Office at Croesyceiliog and of the Libraries at Cwmbran and Newport for their assistance on numerous occasions. They are extremely grateful to the artist Gerard Whyman who provided the illustrations.

This book is dedicated to Mrs. Sylvia Osborne who typed the script of "The Place-Names of Western Gwent" and who would have played a large part in the production of the present book. Her unexpected death on 26th April, 1994 was a shattering blow to her husband and to her many friends. She is sadly missed and very fondly remembered.

Map of Monmouthshir

ohn Speed 1610

SO 301141 (St. Mary's)

Abergavenny (Abergafenni, Y Fenni)

Gobannio(n) (C3)[1], *Aber Geuenni* (1172)[2], *Abergevenni, Abergavenni* (1214)[3], *Bergeueny* (1193-1218)[4] (1245-53)[224], *Bergaven* (c1291)[6], *Bergeveny lordship* (1516)[7], *Venni; p. mair o dref feni* (c1566)[28], *Abergevenny* (1577)[8]

This historic market town stands near the confluence of the Gavenny brook and the river Usk, hence the name, from W *aber* 'mouth of river' and the name *Gavenny (Gafenni).*

The Norman castle dating from about 1090 AD, but rebuilt last century as a hunting lodge, probably stands on the site of the Roman fort *Gobannio(n).* The Normans built a walled town of about 20 acres in extent here; the church of St. Mary (now rebuilt) was originally the chapel of a Benedictine Priory.

The name *Gobannio(n)* which appears in the 3rd Century Antonine Itinerary appears to have come from the British word **gobann* (W *gof)* 'smith', usually 'blacksmith', with the adjectival suffix *io*[1,10], or alternatively from the p.n. *Gobannos*[1] (itself derived from *gobann*).

The river name Gavenny has come from this word *Gobannio(n)*, by vowel affection to *Gevenni*. Under lenition this has become *'evenny'* from which the Welsh Y Fenni appears to have been derived.[11]

The name *Bergavenny* appears to have been introduced by the Normans, apparently under the impression that Abergavenny was, in fact, *'Y Bergavenny;'* the definite article then being lost. Used at; first for the town and Lordship it continued in use as the name of the Hundred.

SO 522004

Barbadoes Hill and Barbadoes Green

Barbadoes Hill (1733)[699]

These places lie above the Wye Valley, to the W of Tintern.

As in the case of *Botany Bay* (which see) this is a transferred name for remote land.[12]

SO 398943

Bertholey (Bertholau)

Bretheli (1223)[13], *Brethelley* (1295)[14], *Berthyllie* (1527)[15], *Bertholie* (1570)[16], *Marthellye Chap* (1577)[8], *Bertholy* (1717)[17].

This name is that of a mansion house belonging to the Kemeys family and of an ancient chapel (now gone) in the lower Usk Valley near Newbridge.

Bradney has proposed a derivation from W *perth* 'bush' and W *goleu* 'light' or 'bright' but 'bright bush' hardly makes sense! An interesting point is that in the earliest forms the second element is *heli* or *elley*; this suggests a derivation from W *helyg* 'willow trees' or possibly the p.n. *Heli*[18] or *Heli(g)*[710] (as in Pwllheli).

The present meaning of W *perth* = *berth* is 'hedge' or 'bush' but one suspects that the original meaning may have been, as in the Cornish language, 'wood'[19] or 'brake' or 'thicket'[20]. So either 'the willow wood or thicket' or 'Heli's wood or thicket'.

SO 362059

Bettws Newydd (Betws Newyd)

Psh. of Bettus Aythan (1432)[21], *Bettus Newith* (1430-47)[22], *Bettehouse filiorum Aythen* (1468-9)[23], *Bettehous Aithan* (1480-1)[24], *Bettows* (1545)[25], *Bettus Newyth* (1545)[26], *Bettus newith* (c1610)[27], *y bettws newyd* (c1566)[28].

Bettws Newydd is near Chain Bridge on the road from Usk to Abergavenny; the church has a notable rood screen.

The name is from W *betws* 'chapel' or 'oratory', a possible borrowing from OE *bed hus* 'beadhouse' or 'oratory', and W *newydd* 'new' i.e. 'the new chapel or oratory'.

Bradney[29] says that the church here was founded by Aeddon ap Gwaethfoel, Lord of Clytha, in 1188 A.D.; this seems to be reflected in some of the name forms.

There is a farm named Bettws about 2 miles North of Bettws Newydd, but nothing seems known of the history of the place.

W *betws* may also mean 'birch grove' and this meaning may be important where there are no ecclesiastical connections. Place-names with W *betws* are found elsewhere in Wales, e.g. Bettws near Newport, Gwent.

SO 537044

Bigsweir

Bykeswere (1295)[30], *Bythicwere* (1306-7)[697], *Bykeleswerr (were)* (1305)[31], (1315)[31], (1436)[31], (1437)[31], *Bikeswere* (1315)[31], (1322)[31], *Bykiswere* (1485-1500)[31], *Bygge Were* (1611)[31], *Bigsweir* (1777)[31].

Bigsweir is actually the name of a weir in the river Wye, also that of a nearby mansion house, approximately 1 mile NW of Llandogo (the mansion house, on the E bank of the Wye, is actually in Gloucestershire). The road along the Wye Valley from Chepstow to Monmouth crosses the river here by an iron bridge (classified as a Monument).

This name has previously been derived from OE *wer* 'weir' and the (unrecorded!) OE p.n. *Biccel* i.e. 'Biccel's Weir'[31]. But Bradney[32] pointed out that a derivation from the W p.n. *Buddig (Buddic)* was possible. Indeed, this seems probable; *Buddig* was reputedly the father of Bishop Oudouceus after whom near-by Llandogo was named.

The name *Buddig* occurs in the nearby place-name Coed Beddick; this place is two miles below Bigsweir and the derivation is from *Buddig* and W *coed* 'wood' i.e. 'Buddig's wood'. Bigsnap Woods, on a hill above the Wye and to the W of Bigsweir may also have taken its name from *Buddig* and OE *cnaep* 'hill-top'.

ST 392875

Bishton (Llangadwaladr Tre Esgob, Trefesgob)

Lann Catgualatyr (c710)[33], (1119)[34], *Bishton manor of Lankaderwader* (1290)[37], *Bishton* (1535)[38], *tre esgob* (c1566)[28], *Bysshеton cast.* (1577)[8], *Biston alias Bishopp's Towne* (1712)[40], *Bishopston* (1833)[41], *Bishton* (1839)[42].

Bishton, a village to the E of Newport, is now in close proximity to the Spencer Steelworks at Llanwern. It was once part of a Manor belonging to the See of Llandaff, hence the name Bishop's Town, from OE *tun*(-ton) 'farm' or 'estate'; this has been contracted to Bishton. The Welsh form from W *tre(f)* 'farm' or 'estate' and W *esgob* 'bishop' means the same thing.

The earliest name is from W *llan* 'church' and the W p.n. *Cadwaladr*[43], i.e. 'Cadwaladr's Church'. The Cadwaladr mentioned here may have been a disciple of St. Cadog[711].

The name Bishton is also found in Gower[44] and in England[45].

SO 522022

Botany Bay

This hamlet is about 1/2 mile NW of Tintern, above the Wye Valley. The name has probably come from that of a field in a outlying part of a farm, hence named after a place regarded at that time as being very distant, e.g. *Botany Bay* (Australia), *Philadelphia* (U.S.A.) etc. Field remarks[39] 'coupled with the idea of distance may be that of hard labour associated with this former penal settlement in New South Wales'.

SO 540001

Brockweir

pull brochuail (c620)[46], *Brocwere, Brokwere* (c1145) (1222) (1270) (1314)[47], *Brockewer* (1248)[47], *Brokewere* (1306)[14], *Brockwere* (1577)[8].

Brockweir, an attractive village, lies on the E bank of the river Wye something over a mile upstream from Tintern. The name has been derived from OE *broc* 'brook' and OE *wer* 'weir' by a number of authorities.[47 48 49]. But the earliest name-form suggests a different origin;[46] *pull brochuail* is from W *pwll* 'pool', here in the sense of 'pool in a river', and the W p.n. *Brochuail*[50] (or Brockmael) i.e. 'Brockmael's pool' (which has become Brockmael's Weir then Brockweir).

Brockmael was a 6th Century Prince of Gwent. His name, from W *broch* 'badger' and W *mael* 'prince' is literally 'badger prince'.

SO 391094

Bryngwyn

Brengwein (1254)[51], *Brangwayn* (c1291)[468], (c1348)[5], *Bryngwyn* (1349-53)[52], *Y bryn gwyn* (c1566)[28], *Broyngwyn* (1570)[53], *Broyngwin* (c1610)[27], *Bryngwvn alias Brengwyn* (1707)[54].

Bryngwyn is a settlement of widely dispersed houses approximately 1 mile NE of Raglan. This area was once part of a grange (monastic farm) belonging to Llantarnam Abbey; before this the Manor of Bryngwyn was part of the Lordship of Abergavenny.

The present name appears to have come from W *bryn* 'hill' and W *gwyn* 'white' or 'fair'. The church stands on a natural elevation. But why 'white' or 'fair'? Moreover, the name-forms are quite variable, though curiously enough, this is also the case with Bryngwyn (Caerwys)[56], Bryngwyn (Herefordshire)[57] and Bryngwyn (Pembrokeshire)[58].

Bradney gives the meaning of this name as 'white mount'[55], but this does not really make sense. This problem also arises in the case of the name *Twyn Gwyn*, a name found quite often in West Gwent; the accepted derivation from W *twyn* 'hillock' and W *gwyn* 'light' or 'fair', again does not really make sense.

The suspicion arises that here, as in Bryngwyn, W *gwyn* is being used in the sense of 'holy' or 'blessed' (as in the Welsh Bible, Gospel of St. Matthew, Ch.5, Verses 3-11) and that there are ecclesiastical associations (were these places 'preaching stations'?) Wakeman has suggested[59] that *Bryngwyn* may have meant, in effect, 'Court of Justice'.

SO 360915

Bulmore

Pelmo(r) (1314)[136], *Pull Mowre* (1535)[38], *Bullmoor* (1624)[124], *Bulmore* (1723)[125].

This place is near Caerleon, on the E bank of the river Usk and upstream; it was the site of a Roman cemetery and the Roman road to Caerleon from the East passed through.

The name appears to have come from W *pwll* and W *mawr*; the latter means 'large' but the former may mean 'pool' (in the river) or 'inlet'. It is not clear which is meant here so 'the big pool' or 'the big inlet' (this could refer to the mouth of the Sor brook).

The name Pill Mawr (again from W *pwll*) is found some three miles downstream from Caerleon, this name has come from a noticeable inlet.

ST 538927

Bulwark or The Bulwarks

This suburb of Chepstow lies near the mouth of the river Wye; the name has come from the Iron Age hillfort[60] nearby.

The term *bulwarks* from ME *bolwerk* 'fortification' is generally used to describe the remains of old fortifications and earthworks.[61]

The name is found elsewhere, being associated with hillforts near Llanmadog *(The Bulwark)*[62] and Porth Kerry *(The Bulwarks)*.[63] It is also found in a Welsh form, i.e. *Y Bwlwarcau* (Llangynwyd)[64]

ST 469905

Caerwent (Caer-went)

Venta Silurum (C3)[68], *Ventaslurum* (c700)[68], *Cair Guent* (943-4)[69], *guentonia urbe* (955)[70], *cairguent* (c1075)[358]: *Caruen, Caroen* (1086)[72], *Chaeruuent* (1165-83)[73], *Kayrewent* (1230-40)[74], *Kaerwent* (c1291)[6], *Caierwent* (1577)[8].

The village of Caerwent lies approximately 10 miles E of Newport and has extensive Roman remains; Caerwent was the provincial capital of the Silures of SE Wales in Roman times.

The earliest name *Venta Silurum* means 'market place of the Silures'[68]. The native Kingdom of Gwent which emerged in C5 following the Roman withdrawal from Britain had *Venta* as its first capital, indeed, the kingdom took its name from the city *(Venta→Guenta)*.

The forms *Cairguent* and *Cairwent* are from OW *cair*, W *caer* 'fort' but sometimes, as here, synonymous with L *civitas* 'town' or 'settlement' and *Venta*, i.e. 'the fort or town called Venta (or Guenta)'.

ST 475883

Caldicot

Caldecote (1086)[72], (1148-83)[76], *Kaldecot* (1222-9)[78], *Caldicote* (1219-29)[77], (1401)[79], *Caldycott* (1577)[8], *Caldicot* (1715)[80].

This town to the W of Chepstow, has an impressive Norman Castle dating to the latter part of C12; the town has been considerably enlarged since the 1960's.

The name is from OE *calde* 'cold' and OE *cot* 'hut' or 'dwelling' meaning 'cold dwelling' or 'cold shelter', i.e. a shelter for travellers. The name Cold Harbour, found quite widely in England, means the same thing (there is a Cold Harbour Pill near Magor).

The name is rare in Wales but is found in several places in England[83] e.g. Caldecote (Bucks), Caldicot (nr. Holt) and Caldicote (Newport Pagnell).

ST 415952

Cas Troggy

Torrogy (1307)[84], *Strogle cast.* (c1610)[27].

This small castle, long ruined, was built by Roger Bigod beside the Troggy brook, to the N of Wentwood. It is sometimes called Striguil though this name has probably arisen as a mis-pronunciation of Cas Troggy (i.e. Strogle) although the little castle was just within the boundary of the Lordship of Striguil (Chepstow).

The name is from W *cas*, diminutive of *castell* 'castle' i.e. 'little castle' and the name of the nearby stream Troggy (*Taroci* (c895))[85].

SO 511027

Catbrook

The village of Catbrook lies about 2 miles S of Trelleck, on a minor road to Tintern. The name is that of a stream nearby which appears in the C12 Book of Llandaff as *Cat-frut*[101]; this from W *cad* 'battle' and W *ffrwd* 'stream' i.e. 'the stream of the battle'. In the modern name W *ffrwd* has been replaced by E *brook*.

ST 373908

Cat's Ash

uillam Cathouen filii hindec (c745)[86], *Catteshasse* (c1113)[87], *Catteshasse* (1289)[88], *Cattes haies* (1299)[89], *Cattesaches* (1355)[88], *Cattisaishe* (1432)[91], *Catch Ashe* (1536)[92], *Catsasthe* (1585)[93].

This hamlet near Llanbedr, at the W end of Wentwood, is the site of an ancient settlement. Charles[88] gives the meaning of the name as 'the wild cat's ash tree' though this seems a little odd.

In fact it is clear from the earliest name-form that Cathouen, described as *filii hindec* i.e. 'the son of Hindec' is a personal name. There is some doubt as to whether the sixth letter of *Cathouen* is u, as written, or *n* (the two are not infrequently confused in old manuscripts). The latter would give *Cathonen* literally 'Cat's Ash' from W *cath* 'Cat' and W *onnen* 'Ash Tree'.

Intermediate forms tend to be from OE *aesc* 'ash tree'.

ST 440913

Cayo (Caeau)

Caya farm (1790)[65]

The above name-form is that of a farm in the parish of Llanvaches. But the name is found in several other places in Gwent and elsewhere in Wales, e.g. Cayo (Carms.)[66] and Caeau (Flint)[67].

The derivation is from W *cae*, plural *caeau*, originally 'hedge' or 'fence' then 'that enclosed by such' i.e. 'enclosure'.

It is often associated with old walled or enclosed settlements. Later on, W *cae* came to mean simply 'field'.

Chepstow (Cas-gwent)

ST 535930

Emricorua in guent iscoit (c722)[94], *Castellum de Estrighoiel or Strigoielg* (1086)[75], *castellguent* (1128)[35], (1129)[36], *Striguill* (1254)[277], *Storguyl* (c1291)[6], *Chepstowe* (1308)[95], *Cheppistowe* (1535)[38], *Chepstow* (1577)[8].

This historic market town lies at the mouth of the Wye, on the border between Gwent and Gloucestershire. The impressive Norman Castle (parts dating from 1071 AD) was the first stone castle to be built in Wales; it became the administrative centre for the Marcher Lordship of Striguil, later Chepstow.

Chepstow has been a walled town since the 13th century. The principal church, a Norman foundation, was originally the Chapel of a Benedictive Priory. It has been suggested[96] that the earliest name *Emricorua (Emricorfa)* is from W *amrygyr* 'busy' and W *fa* 'place' i.e. 'busy place' in the sense of emporium; Chepstow appears to have taken the place of Caerwent as the 'market place' of the region.

The Norman name for Chepstow was *Striguil (Estrighoel)* a name which may well have come from W *ystraigl* 'river bend'[97]. There is a particularly sharp bend in the Wye to the North of the present castle. This was also the site of an Iron Age hill-fort[98] and the name may have originated here.

The name Chepstow is from OE *ceap* 'market' and OE *stowe*[99, 100] 'place of assembly' i.e. 'market place'.

ST 347894

Christchurch, Newport (Eglwys y Drindod)

sancte Trinitatis (1204)[273] *sancte Trinitatis iuxta Karlion* (1230-40)[274], *Cristeschurch* (1254)[347], *Sanctae Trinitatis* (1290)[87], *Cristeschurche* (c1291)[468], *Christchurch in the Wode* (1349)[102], *eglwys y drindod* (c1566)[28].

Now a suburb of Newport, on the hills to the E of the town, the name has come from the church which is in a commanding position on a ridge at the W end of Wentwood. This was once the church for the Commotes of Lebeneth and Edlogan, so the present parish represents a great reduction in size.

The name is, of course, 'Church of Christ' (though the dedication is to the Holy Trinity; the early name-form *Sancte Trinitas* is from L *sanctus* 'holy' and L *trinitas* 'Trinity').

SO 368094
(chapel farm)

Clytha (Cleidda)

Kylitha (1256)[103], *Killithan* (1312-13)[127], *Killithan* (1430-7)[22], (1596)[105], *toyne Clitha* (1601)[107], *Clytha* (1545)[108], *Clitha* (1595) [109], *hamlet of Clytha* (1731)[110].

This name is that of a mansion house (Clytha Court) and of scattered houses within the parish of Llanarth; there was once a chapel here and the remains are believed to have been incorporated in Chapel Farm.

Bradney[111] says that the place-name is derived from a personal name ('from the giant *Clytha*'). But the first element appears to be W *cil* 'retreat' or hermitage' and Wakeman[112] has proposed a derivation from *cil* and the p.n. *Ithan (Aeddon?)* i.e. *'Ithan's (Aeddon's)* retreat'. Aeddon ap Gwaithfoed was Lord of Clytha in 1188.

Chapel Farm near Clytha Park apparently takes its name from Capel Aeddan (SO 374093), the site of which is nearby.

Coldra

ST 357903

Coudrey (1100-35)[114], *Coudray* (c1291)[468], *Coudre* (1322)[696], *Cowldre* (1566)[115], *Coldrey* (1596-7)[116], *Coeldrey* (1659)[117], *manor of Coldry* (1699)[118].

Once a manor of Goldcliff Priory, this name became that of a farm and then of houses to the E of Newport.

It should be noted that in early name-forms the *'l'* in this word is consistently missing, otherwise a derivation from W *col* 'peak'[119] or extreme point[120] might seem to be indicated.

The most likely derivation is from W *cordref* 'small estate or settlement'.

The Cot

ST 505991

This is a hamlet appoximately 2 miles SW of Tintern. The name is from OE *cot* 'hut', 'shelter' or 'cottage'.

SO 510047

Cotland

The hamlet of Cotland lies approximately 1 mile SE of Trelleck. The name is from *cotland* 'small piece of arable land held with a *cot*'[121]

ST 483997

Creigau (Creigiau)

This hamlet lies to the N of Devauden. The name is from W *crug* (plural *crugiau*) 'mound(s)' i.e. 'the mounds'.

The name is found elsewhere e.g. Creigau nr. Cardiff

ST 488902

Crick (Crug)

Villa carnou id est uilla crucov leuirn(?) (c1022)[123], *Villam sancti Nuuien cum ecclesia* (1119)[34], (1128)[35], (1129)[36], *Kric* (1245-53)[129], *le Crick munede* (late c13)[130], *Creke* (c1610)[27], *Crick* (1787)[131].

The village of Crick lies to the E of Caerwent on the road to Chepstow. The name is from British *cruc*, 'mound' from which both W *crug* and OE *cryc* appear to have come.

Early name-forms indicate that there was once a chapel here dedicated to St. Nevyn[132] (Nuvien); this is said to have become a cowshed on Crick Manor Farm.

The name has come from the Middle Bronze Age barrow on the North side of the A48, approximately 1/4 mile to the West of the present village[133].

Cwmcarvan (Cwmcarfan)

S0 478075

Concauvern (1148-86)[346], *Cumkarvan* (1314)[136], *ecclesia de Cumcaruan* (c1348)[106], *Comcarvan* (1415)[135], *Comcaruan* (c1610)[27].

This very small hamlet with a church lies in a secluded country position some five miles to the E of Raglan. The name has been taken from the valley of the little river Carfan (a tributary of the Trothy (Troddi) in which the place lies.

The first element is thus W *cwm* 'valley'. The second element *carfan* or *carvan* is also found in the better-known Llancarvan (Llancarfan) near Cowbridge and the origin of this element has been considered at length[245].

On the basis of a legend recounted in the Vita Sancti Cadoci[137], Nant Carfan (the earlier name for Llancarfan) has been derived from W *nant* ('brook' in modern Welsh but occasionally 'valley') and W *carw* 'stag' i.e. 'the Stag's Valley'. But the underlying story is clearly apocryphal and Thomas[138] has suggested that *carfan* may mean 'line' or 'boundary' or alternatively, that it is a personal name.

This latter suggestion has been made elsewhere and there is some evidence to support it.[99, 140]

Cwmyoy (Cwm-iau)

S0299233

Cunnou (1131)[141], *Connuouir* (1147)[142], *Comuy, Comyow* (1527)[701], *Cwmyoye* (1547-51)[143], *Comyove* (1591-2)[144], *Camyoye* (1591-2)[145]

The hamlet of Cwmyoy with its church is situated around the mouth of the valley of a little tributary of the Honddu brook, some 3 miles to the S of Llanthony Abbey; this was once a grange of the Abbey.

The derivation of the name which seems to have been accepted [146, 147] is from W cwm 'valley' and W *iau* (OW *iou*) 'yoke'; from a distant aspect the valley has a shape somewhat reminisent of an old-fashioned yoke. But it is of interest that the not too dissimilar *'Cymmyou'* is found elsewhere[691, 692] and, here, this has been interpreted as a form of *cymau* (a plural of W *cwm*) meaning '(the) valleys'.

Such an interpretation makes sense here, too. The settlement at Cymyoy stands at the junction of two valleys and the name may then have been given to the side valley, itself. It is of interest that the name of the stream actually running through the valley now known as Cwm Iau seems not to have been evidenced in early forms.

ST 484988

Devauden

de vske iux (ta.....de) vauden (c14)[151], *Devawden* (1464)[152], *Tee ir Vawden* (1506)[153], *the Vawden in Newchurch* (1567)[154]

The village of Devauden lies approximately 4 miles N of Chepstow on the road to Monmouth (B4293).

The second element in the name is W *ffawydden* 'beech tree'. The first element is possibly less immediately apparent. The name-form *Tee ir Vawden* (1506) appears to be *Tŷ'r ffawydden* 'house of the beech tree' and in the following form *'tŷ'r'* may well have been anglicised to *'the'*.

Bradney[155] records the names *Y Dyfawden* and *Dyfawden* for land (not in Devauden) 'between the Lordships of Edlogan and Tregrug' and it is apparently from a similar name-form that Devauden has come. In Y Dyfawden, W *tŷ* 'house' appears to have become *dy*, giving, as in Devauden, the meaning 'house of (or near) the beech tree'.

ST 467889

Dewstow

Sanctum Dewin (1086)[72], *capella sancti Dauid* (1165-83)[156], *Capellam sancti Dauid* (1186-91)[157], *Dewystowe* (post 1250)[158], *(vill of Deuestowe* (1290)[159], *Deuston* (1577)[8], *parish of Caldicot, Manor of Dewstow(e),* (1715)[160]

This was once a Manor, with a chapel (long gone) near Caldicot. The name is retained in Dewstow House.

Dewstow is from the Welsh p.n. *Dewi* 'David' and OE *stowe* 'meeting place', used here in a religious sense and equivalent to W *llan* 'church' so 'Church of St. David'[82]. The name *Dewstowe* also occurs in Cornwall. The Welsh equivalent is Llanddewi.

S0 458101

Dingestowe (Llanddingad)

Ecclesia Dincat, (c872)[162], *Villam merthirdincat cum ecclesia* (1119)[34], *Landinegat* (1193-1218 or 1254)[163], *Ecclesia de Landenegath* (1254)[51], *Denstowe* (1290)[164], *Dingestowe* (1453)[166], *Landynggatte* (1457)[167], *Dyngastow* (1464)[165], *Dingestow* (c1610)[27].

This village lies on the river Trothy (Troddi) some 4 miles E of Raglan, on the Monmouth road. The name is that of the church which was reputedly founded by Dingat in the 6th Century[168].

Earliest forms are from L *ecclesia* 'church' and from W *merthyr* 'church' (in the sense of a place associated with a martyr). In later forms W *llan* 'church' appears then this is replaced by OE *stowe* 'place of assembly' but here also meaning 'church'. All forms thus mean 'Church of St. Dingat'. Dingat was a son of Brychan, King of Brycheiniog.

ST 481923 (Castle)

Dinham

Dinan (1086)[72], *Dinan* (1193-1218)[128], *Dinham* (1271)[171], *Dinas* (1321-2)[172], *Dynan* (1329)[173], *Dynam* (1567)[174], *Dynham* (1577)[8].

This site of a small castle, S of Shirenewton bears the same name as a nearby farm. Dinham (Dinan) is mentioned in the Domesday Book as a 'hardwick' (dairy farm).

The name is from W *din* 'fortress' with the diminutive suffix *an* i.e. 'the small fortress or castle'. It has been anglicised, the second element *an* having become *ham*, reminiscent of OE *ham* 'home', indeed, Bradney[171] gives this derivation.

The *Cestill Dinan*[35, 175] mentioned in the Book of Llandaff appears to be Bishton castle not Dinham.

The name is found elsewhere[176] e.g. Dinam, Anglesey and Dinan or Dinam in Brittany.

Dixton (Llanddidwg)

SO 520136

Ecclesia Tytiuc super ripam guy, podium bennlann (glossed) .I. eccl'a tituuc (c735)[177], *bennlann titiuc* (c886)[178], *Lanntydiuc* (1056-63)[179], *Sancto Tedeoco* (1134-48)[180], *Dukeston* (c1291)[266], *Duxton* (1425)[181], *Dixton* (c1610)[27].

The village of Dixton lies approximately 1 mile NE of Monmouth, on the road to Ross. The earliest name-form is from L *ecclesia* 'church' and the p.n. *Diwg*[182], the name is preceded by the hypocoristic or honorific title W *ty* (te) to give *Tytiuc*. In later forms L *ecclesia* is replaced by W *llan* and then OE *tun* (-ton) 'enclosure' but used here in the same sense as *llan* i.e. 'church'. All name-forms mean 'Church of St. Diwg'.

Earlswood

ST 455950

Erleswod (1443)[183], *Erles Woode* (c1610)[27], *litle forest called Earles Woode* (1613)[184], *coed y yarlle* (1630)[185].

This is the name of an area of widely dispersed houses and farms some 3 miles NW of Shirenewton. It was once a small forest, part of the Lordship of Caldicot, a one-time possession of the Earls of Hereford, hence the name[184].

Gaer fawr

ST 442985

Gayr Vowor, Kayr Vawour (1488)[700], *Gare Vawr* (1725)[186].

The hamlet of Gaer fawr lies approximately 2 miles SE of Llangwm, on a minor road. The name has come from the large hill-fort nearby i.e. from W *caer* = *gaer* 'hillfort', in this case, and W *mawr* = *fawr* 'large' i.e. 'the large hill-fort'.

ST 448968

(*) Gaerllwvd (Gaer-lwyd)

Garne Lloyde (1613)[187], *Gair loyd* (1665)[188].

This hamlet is near a crossroads on the road (B4235) between Usk and Chepstow. The original name Garn Lwyd comes from a Neolithic long barrow or burial chamber, the remains of which may be seen by the roadside (on private land); the name is from W *carn* = *garn* 'mound' or 'pile of stones' (i.e. the long barrow), and W *llwyd* = *lwyd.* This last word is ordinarily translated 'grey' or 'pale'. But the meaning here seems to be 'sacred' or 'connected with the supernatural'.

Over the years W *garn* has become W *caer* = *gaer* (actually 'hill-fort') probably by association with nearby Gaer fawr though Gaer lwyd is not appropriate.

(*) This is the spelling on the 1" O.S. map. It is incorrect, see W form.

ST 366831

Goldcliff (Allt euryn)

Goldcliue (1120)[189], *Gholcliue* (1186-91)[190], *Golcliue* (1186-91)[191], *Goldclive* (1214)[192], (1254)[347], *Golclivia* (1229)[193], *Goldclif* (1245-53)[194], *Golcliuam Golcl(iua)* (1236-40)[195], *Golcleff* (1415)[196], *Golclyf* (1529-32)[197], *Goldeclyffe* (1577)[8].

The village of Goldcliff lies near the E bank of the estuary at the River Usk, near sea-coast cliffs from which the name appears to have come. It is also the site of a Benedictine Priory founded here in 1113 A.D.

A derivation of the name from OE *gold* 'gold' and OE *clyf* 'cliff' has achieved considerable currency[198]. In his *Itinerarium*

Cambriae (written circa 1214 A.D.) which describes his journey through Wales in 1188 A.D. Giraldus says:

> 'Not far hence there stands a rock on the sea overhanging the waves of the Severn called by the English Gouldcliffe, that is to say, a golden rock because it exhibits stones of a golden colour reflecting the rays of the sun and glittering with a wonderful brightness'.

A rationale for this was provided by the geologists Buckland and Conybeare who remarked, in 1824[199] 'The name of Goldcliff is derived from the iron pyrites in the lias'. Later on, in 1893, H. B. Woodward[200] wrote 'The name Gold Cliff was derived from the glittering appearance of the iron pyrites formerly to be seen in the black (Rhaetic) Shales'.

The sea cliff at Goldcliff has been faced with masonry since 1824. However, in 1905 there was a break in the wall; this allowed Richardson[201] to record a succession in the Lower Lias, Rhaetic and Keuper measures.

Iron pyrites would be expected to occur in these measures. But iron pyrites when exposed to the elements oxidises rapidly and, in fact, only irregular ferruginous nodules were found. Moreover, rocks with a greenish-yellow colour, i.e. the greenish yellow shales, represented only 12.29% of the total thickness.

Thus, although it is clearly not possible to say with certainty what geological conditions were like at the time of Giraldus' Itinerary, there seems to be the distinct possibility that Giraldus's account was not just an exaggeration, but was more or less a product of the imagination!

After all, the geology of the strata at Lavernock Point is generally similar to that at Goldcliff, but phenomena as described by

Giraldus have never been associated with this place or with other geologically similar places nearby.

In some of the name-forms the first element is *ghol* or *gol* not *gold*. It is difficult to assess the significance of this since, in place-names, *gol* is sometimes encountered as an abbreviated form of *gold*, (as, for instance, in *Golbourne*)[202]. A stream runs into the sea near Goldcliff and a derivation for OE *goule* ME *gole* 'stream' cannot be entirely dismissed.

But there may be a clue in the words of Giraldus 'called by the English Gouldcliffe'; this suggests a different W name. McClure[328] has proposed that the original name was from W *gallt* 'cliff'. This could have given rise to the hybrid name '*gallt* cliff' (from OE *clyf*) which became Goldcliff. Legends then grew up to explain the name.

SO 448128

Grace Dieu

monasterium Beatae Mariae de Gratia Dei (1125)[203], *Grace Dieu* (1236)[204], *Abbas de gratia dei* (c1348)[205], *Gras dew* (1535)[38], *Gracedue* (c1610)[27], *Grace Dieu* (c1790)[206].

Grace Dieu was a Cistercian Monastery built in 1226 by John of Monmouth on a site near what is now Llanvihangel Ystern Llewern. The Monastery was not tolerated locally and was soon destroyed, but rebuilt some seven years later on a site across the Trothy (Troddi). Nothing is to be seen there now, but the name which is retained in Parc Grace Dieu is from L *gratia dei*, Norman-French Grace Dieu, 'Thanks to God'.

Grosmont (Y Grysmwnt)

SO 245404

Forest of Crassomonte (1148-83)[346], *Grossi Montis* (1254)[113], *Grossomonte Grosmund* (1256-7)[208], *Grosse Monte* (c1291)[6], *De ecclesia de Grosemond* (c1245-53)[224], *Grossmont* (1529)[209], *Grosmont* (1556-8)[211], (1836)[212], *y grysmwnt* (c1566)[28], *Grossemont* (1592)[210].

This small town is on the River Monnow, on the border with Herefordshire. There is an impressive Norman Castle; in medieval times this place was an important borough.

The name is from NF *grosse monte* 'big hill or mountain'[213] which is appropriate because Grosmont lies at the foot of a prominent hill. Nevertheless, the name is probably an importation from France; the Cistercian Abbey of the same name in the North Riding of Yorkshire is named after the French mother house[214].

Gwehelog

SO 388045

Wellok (1295)[14], *Argoyt Welok* (1314)[136], *Wehelok* (1420)[215], *Gwehelocke* (1581)[216], *Gweyne Goheloge* (1547)[217], *Gwehelog, Guehellogg* (1743)[218].

Gwehelog is a village with the houses dispersed widely, some three miles N of Usk town.

The Welsh word *gwely* was used to denote 'free' people claiming a common ancestry and living on hereditary land *(tir gwelyog)* The name is derived from W *gwely* with the adjectival ending *og*, i.e. *gwelyog* 'place with *gwely* settlements'.

SO 415017

Gwernesney (Gwernesni)

Warnesty (1295)[14], *Warnsti* (1314)[136], *Warnestny* (c1348)[106], *Gwernesny* (1535)[220], *Gwernessenye* (1577)[8], *Gwernessney* (1658)[221].

This village lies approximately 2 miles E of Usk town. The name is from W *gwern* 'alders' (signifying swampy land) and the p.n. *Esni* i.e. 'Esni's alder marsh'. Esni was an early Dean of Llandaff; he was the brother of Bishop Urban[222]. This p.n. is also found in Rhosesni in Denbighshire[223].

Hardwick

Herdewyk (1361)[572], *Hardwike* (1535)[38], *Hardwick chap* (1577)[8].

This name is found in several parts of Gwent and elsewhere e.g. Hardwick Nr. Abergavenny, Hardwick Nr. Chepstow, Hardwick Farm St. Brides Netherwent etc.

The name is from OE *heordewic*, generally 'dairy farm'[225].

ST 399915

Hendrew

Lannpetyr in hennriu (c1045)[226], *uillam henriu cum ecclesia* (1128)[35], *Henru* (1361)[227], *Manor of Masegwenyth or Henrewe* (1582)[229], *Hendrew* (1836)[212].

This was once a medieval manor, the name is retained as a farm name; the place lies to the E of Llanbedr.

The name is from W *hen* 'old' and W *rhiw* 'ascent' i.e. 'hillside with a track', usually an ancient way. An extraneous *d* has been introduced into the name fairly recently.

Henrhiw is also the name of a farm near Monkswood, on the Usk to Pontypool road; this is also near an ancient trackway.

ST 502955

Howick (Yr Hywig)

ecclesiam Guruid cum sua tellure (c660)[230], *sancto Gormasii* (1193-1218)[128], *Howich* (1193-1218)[128], *sancto Wormeto, Howyk* (1223)[231], *ecclesia de sancto Wo(r)meto* (c1348)[232], *Howykke* (1536)[233], *howic fach* (1566)[9], *Howick* (1577)[8].

This is now the name of a farm situated about 2½ miles NW of Chepstow; the ancient chapel of St. Wormet was probably nearby.

The earliest name-form is from L *ecclesia* 'church' and the p.n. *Guruid*, the name of a saint, which also appears in the forms *Gurmaet* and *Wormet*[234]. This has been associated with Howick[235].

The name Howick is from OE *hoh* 'ridge' and OE *wic* 'farm'[237] i.e. 'the farm on the ridge'; this is topographically appropriate. The name is found elsewhere[198].

ST 467879

Ifton (Ifftwn)

Yueton (1193-1218)[128], (c1348)[238], *Iuetone* (1270)[239], *Yefton* (1535)[628], *Ifftwn* (c1566)[28], *Ifton* (1577)[8], *Ufton* (1598)[240].

Once a manor with an ancient church (now gone), the name is retained in Ifton Manor (House) near Caldicot.

The name has been derived from the OE p.n. *Ifa* and OE *tun (-ton)* 'farm' or 'estate' i.e. 'Ifa's estate'[241]. But the Welsh p.n. *Iudon* is a more likely source. Iudon[242] (where *u* is probably written for *v*) is an early form of the W p.n. *Iddon*[243]; King Iddon was the son of Ynyr Gwent, King of Gwent in the 6th Century and the name is associated with land grants in this area, for instance, Uidon, described as 'hereditarius filius of Ithael rex' is mentioned in the grant of *Villa Guinnonui* (this was near Mounton)[698].

ST 493953

Itton (Llanddeiniol)

ecclesiam Diniul (c860)[244], *Hudeton* (1254)[277], *Oditon* (1270)[239], *Editon* (1271)[245], *Hedyngton* (1306)[227], *Edeton* (c1291)[402], *ecclesia de Eodeton* (c1348)[238], *Itton* (1468)[246], *Ytton* (1535)[38], (1625)[247].

Itton village lies 3 miles W of Chepstow, on the road to Monmouth (B4293). Itton Court Mansion has a 14/15th Century gatehouse, all that remains of an earlier mansion.

The earliest name-form, from L *ecclesia* 'Church' and the W p.n. *Dinuil* or *Deiniol* = *Ddeiniol*, 'Daniel' suggests that the first chapel hereabouts was founded by a Deiniol, possibly the son of the Abbot of Bangor-is-coed Nr. Chester, hence the W form.

Charles[248] has suggested, rather unconvincingly, a derivation of the name Itton from 'the OE p.n's *Eodbald* or *Eoduald* or, alternatively, from the O.German p.n. *Eudo*'. But it seems more likely that the name has come from the W p.n. *Aidan* (diminutive of *Aed*)[514]. Hedynton (1306) appears to be an anglicised form of *Aidan* and OE *tun (ton)* 'estate' and other forms are a contraction of this or have arisen from *Aed* (or its alternative forms *Oed* and *Haodh*)[249].

At least three W saints are known with the name Aidan and one of these was a companion of St. Dyfrig.

SO 349048

Kemeys Commander

Ecclesia de Kemmeys, Templariorum (1254)[113], *Kemis Comaunder* (c1610)[27].

This hamlet with a church lies approximately 5 miles NW of Usk town, on the Abergavenny road; the place is on the banks of the River Usk, near a pronounced bend in the river.

It is not clear whether the name has come from this river bend (W *cemais*) or from the Kemeys family (see Kemeys Inferior).

The church was at one time under the patronage of the Knights Templar. They called their house and possessions a Commandery and this has given rise to the second part of the place-name. All records concerning the early history of the Church appear to have been lost.

ST 381928

Kemeys Inferior (Cemais)

Cemeis (c700)[252], *cemeis* (c755)[253], *Kameys* (1254)[495], *Clammeys* (c1291)[6], *Kemmeys* (1314)[136], (1423)[254], *kemais* (c1566)[28], *Kemis* (1577)[8].

Once apparently the site of an ancient settlement but now a manor house and church site, with some houses, on the E bank of the River Usk, some 3 miles NE of Caerleon. The river makes a series of very sharp bends hereabouts.

The name is apparently from W *cemais* 'bend(s) or loop(s) in a river'[255]; inferior (ex L *inferior*) is used in the sense of 'lower', to distinguish the place from Kemeys upstream (Kemeys Commander). Kemeys is also a family name (taken from the place).

Cemais (Kemeys) was also the name of a Marcher Lordship, then Hundred in Pembrokeshire[256, 257].

ST 454912

Kilgwrrwg (Cilgwrwg)

Cumcerruc ....uillam que fuit guroc (c722)[258], *Kilcorruc* (1254)[495], *Gilgurrock* (1295)[14], *Kilgorroc* (1348)[106], *Gilkorroc* (1411)[259], *Kilgyruc* (c1566)[9], *Kilgwrrwg* (1833)[41].

Now the name of an isolated chapel on an ancient site approximately 2 miles SW of Devauden; Kilgwrrwg House and Common are nearby.

The name is from W *cil* 'retreat' or 'hermitage' and the W p.n. *Gwrwg's* (Gwrrwg's) retreat'.

ST 534965

Lancaut

lannceuid (c635)[261], *podum ceuid* (c703)[262], *Landcawet* (1061-5)[263], *Lancaut* (1361)[227], *lancant chap (el)* (1610)[27].

The Lancaut Peninsula, to the N of Chepstow and on the E bank of the River Wye, is almost encircled by a massive loop in the river.

It takes its name from an early church, i.e from W *llan* 'church' and the p.n. *Cewydd* i.e. 'Church of St. Cewydd'[264].

Cewydd was a Welsh saint with the reputed ability to influence the weather[264]. His festival day was on July 1st. If it rained on that day it was believed that a rainy period would follow (c.f. English St. Swithin).

ST 375900

Langstone

ad lapidem longum (c940)[134], *langeston* (1193-1218 or 1254)[163], *Langestone* (1314)[136], *ecclesia de Langeston* (c1348)[238], *Langston* (1535)[38], *Langstone* (1836)[212].

This is a village to the E of Newport. Although some name-forms have no terminal *e*, this name has clearly come from OE *ston* 'stone' (as indicated by the earliest name-form, not from OE *tun (-ton)* 'estate or farm'.

The earliest name-form is from L *lapis* (lapidem) 'stone' and L *longum* 'long' or 'tall', i.e. 'the long stone'. This stone, no longer standing, is in a field near Langstone Court, adjacent to the M4 road.

The name is found in England, e.g. Langstone, Hants.[139] (Langeston, 1324).

Langstone; the recumbent "long stone".

Liswerry (Llyswyry)

ST 345875

Liswiry (1290)[265], *Leswyrye* (1295)[14], *Leswyry* (1314)[14], *Llyswiri* (1583)[267], *Liswery* (1636)[268], *Llyswerry* (1653)[269].

Liswerry is now a suburb of Newport, on the E bank of the River Usk. But it was once the *llys* or 'court' from which the Commote of Lebeneth (the lowlands to the E of Newport) was governed.

The first element in the name is quite clear; it is W *llys* 'court'. But the second element has generated controversy.

A derivation from W *(g)wyry* has been suggested[270] and, indeed, looks likely. But if we take *(g)wyry* to mean 'maiden' ('maidens' has been suggested) this does not seem to make much sense. However, *(g)wyry* also means 'virgin' and this may refer to an actual person. Cein (Ceinwen), one of the 'daughters' of Brychan, King of Brycheiniog, was known as Ceinwyry 'St Kein the virgin'[271]. She appears to have been known in the area. For instance, Machen (Machein) is from W *Ma* 'place' and this p.n. *Cein*, and there may be a reference to her in this name Liswerry.

Phillimore has suggested a derivation from the W female p.n. *Ywerydd*[275].

Livox (Llwyfos or Llyfos)

ST 537975

Ken llevos (1415)[276], *Coyde a lloyvos* (1567)[154], *(*), Coid Lluas* (1593)[278], *(*), Coed Llyfos* (1697)[279], *(*)*.

Livox is the name of houses, a farm and a quarry on the peninsula formed by the curving Wye below the Wyndcliff. On the current 2" 0.S. map the name of the farm appears as Liveoaks and it has been suggested[280] that Livox is derived from this. In fact, the reverse appears to be the case and Livox seems to be a form of W *llwyfos* the plural of W *llwyfen* 'elm tree', so 'the elm trees' or 'the elm grove'[281].

It is of interest that there is a reference[282] to 'the Elms lands, once Llivos..' on Grange Farm, Llantilio Crossenny.

(*) These refer to Coed Ll(w)yfos, Shirenewton.

SO 376109

Llanarth (Llan-arth)

Lanngarth (c600)[283], *mainaur Lann Garth* (c720)[284], *apud lanngarth* (c864)[285], *Lanhart* (1193-1218 or 1254)[163], *Lanarch* (c1291)[6], *Llannarthe* (1514)[286], *Llanarthe* (c1610)[27], *Lanarth* (1787)[131].

This village lies approximately 3 miles NW of Raglan; the name is that of the church, i.e. from W *llan* 'church' and W *garth* = *arth* 'hill' or 'rising land' (the church stands on a mound about 30 ft above the generally level surface of Llanarth Court grounds).

Note that whereas in Modern Welsh, *llan* being a feminine noun requires the mutation *garth*→*arth*, in the earliest name-forms this mutation does not occur.

ST 371891

Llanbedr (Llan-bedr)

Lannpetyr in Hennriu (c1045)[288], *Llanbed* (1577)[8], *Llanbedr* (1584)[289], *Llambeder* (1695)[290].

The village of Llanbedr lies to the E of Newport, beyond Langstone. The name is that of an ancient church once situated on a ridge to the N of the present village, but of which no traces now remain.

The name is from W *llan* 'church' and *Petr* = *Bedr* 'Peter', i.e. 'Church of St. Peter'.

S0 371022

Llancayo (Llancaeo)

Llan Kayo (1535)[38], *Lankayo* (1559)[291], *Llancayo* (1591)[292], *Llancaio* (1617)[293].

This is the name of a farm and some houses about 1½ miles N of Usk town; a ruined windmill is a prominent landmark hereabouts.

This name poses problems. There seems to be no evidence that there was ever a church in this locality. In such cases W *llan* is often found to have come from W *(g)lan* 'bank or edge of river'. But Llancayo is not on the banks of the Cayo stream; Cwmcayo is a different valley, the next one to the S!

However, W *glan* may also mean 'hillock' or 'mountainside', indeed the hill separating Llancayo from the valley of the Cayo is named Llancaeo Hill. It seems likely that the hill was originally Lancaeo, and that the farm and village name has come from the hill *(lan→llan)*. *Cayo* has come from W *caeau* (pl. of *cae*) "enclosures".

Llanddewi Fach

There are two churches of this name in Gwent. One is near Llandegveth in W Gwent. The other, near Caldicot, is more widely known as Dewstow (which see).

The name is from W *Dewi* = *Ddewi* 'David' and W *bach* = *fach* 'small' i.e. 'the little Church of St. David'. Note that Llanddewi is sometimes anglicised and written, as pronounced, Llanthewy.

SO 350129

Llanddewi Rhydderch

Landewy (1254)[51], *De ecclesia de Landewy Ruthery* (c1348)[5], *Llanddewi Rhydderch* (1540)[295], *Llanthewy Rithergh* (1573)[296], *Lanthewyrytbirch* (1577)[8], *Llanddwy Rytherch* (1787)[131].

This village lies approximately 4 miles E of Abergavenny, on a minor road. The name is that of the church i.e. from W *llan* 'church' *Dewi* = *Ddewi* 'David', also from the W p.n. *Rhydderch* (name of a place, too). Churches dedicated to St. David are found in many places in Wales, so distinguishing suffixes are often added. In this case this is Rhydderch.

It is not known which person named Rhydderch is commemorated here. Two obvious candidates are: Rhydderch ap Caradog, King of Ewyas and Gwent[297], and King Rhydderch ap Iestyn whose name appears in the Llandaff Charters.

SO 341170

Llanddewi Skirrid (Llanddewi Ysgyryd)

Landewisciret (1254)[51], *ecclesia de Landewy skyret* (c1348)[5], *ll dewi ysgyryd* (c1566)[28], *Llanthewyskirid* (1610)[27].

The hamlet of Llanddewi Skirrid is some 3 miles E of Abergavenny, at the foot of the Skirrid mountain. The name is that of the church, i.e. from W *llan* 'church', *Dewi* = *Ddewi* 'David' and the name of the mountain, Skirrid, (from W *ysgyryd* 'broken' or 'shattered', referring to the irregular shape).

So 'Church of St. David (near the) Skirrid'.

S0 416039

Llandenny (Llandenni)

mathenni (c760)[298], (c785)[299], *Mahenni* (1254)[495], *Mykenny* (c1291)[6], *Mathenny* (1295)[14], *Mathenny* (1314)[136], *Landenny* (1535)[38], *Llandenye* (1577)[8], *Landennie* (1608)[300].

Llandenny village is some six miles NE of Usk town, off the Raglan road. The earliest name-forms are from W *ma* 'place (of)' and the p.n. *Tenni* or *Denni*[301]. In later forms, W *ma* has been replaced by W *llan* 'church', so 'Church of St. Tenni'.

In the earliest name-form Mathenni is described as *Mistuir Mawr* i.e. 'the great monastery'. This suggests the presence here, in pre-Norman times, of an important foundation of the 'Celtic' Church.

ST 401903

Llandevaud

Villam sancti Tyuauc (1119)[34], *SS. Tidauc and Tatan* (1127)[302], *uillam sancti tauauc cum ecclesia* (1128)[35], *Landevok Landevack* (1455)[303], *Landavauk* (1583-4)[304].

This village is approximately 3 miles E of Newport. The name has come from the church i.e. from W *llan* 'church' and the W p.n. *Tavauc*[305], so 'Church of St. Tavauc'.

There was a Lann Tiuauc[306] (c1035) in Glamorgan (Penychen).

ST 411871

Llandevenny

Landenenyon (1314)[136], *Llandevenew* (1542)[307], *Llandevenen* (1674)[308].

The hamlet of Llandevenny is in the parish of St. Brides Netherwent, 1 mile W of Magor. The name is that of a church no longer in existence, though a farm in the district is called 'The Chapel' and this may mark the church site.

The name is from W *llan* 'church' and the p.n. *Gwenny*, a form of Winwaloe[309]. Under mutation *Gwenny* has become *Wenny* and the honorific or hypocoristic title W ty *(te)* has been added as a prefix to give Llandevenny 'Church of St. Gwenny'.

There is a Landevennie in Brittany.

Llandogo

SO 527041

lann enniaun (c625)[310], *Lannenniaun (glossed) lannoudocui* (c698)[311], *Landigo* (1254)[495], *Lanthogo* (c1291)[6], *Llandogo* (1577)[8].

This village on the River Wye lies approximately 3 miles N of Tintern. The name has been taken from the church, originally from W *llan* 'church' and the p.n. *Enniaun (Ennion);* this may well have been the *Einniaun,* an early King of Glywysing who gave land here to *St. Dubricus (Dyfrig), St. Telavius (Teilo)* and to Bishop *Oudouceus* of Llandaff. The latter founded a Monastery here which was named after him, e.g. *Lannoudoci→Llaneuddogwy→ Llandogo.* He is reputed to have died here in 615 A.D.[312]

Llanerthill (Llanefrddyl)

SO 431045

Lann Emrdil, Lannefrdil (c685)[313], *Llanerthil* (1746)[314], *Lanerhill* (1839)[42].

This place is in the parish of Llandenny, about 3 miles N of Llandenny Church. There was once a chapel here, but this has been long gone and the name is now that of a mansion house is from W *llan* 'church' and the p.n. *Efrddyl (Efrdyl)*[316] so St 'Church of St. Efrddyl'. St. Efrddyl was the mother of St. Dyfrig.

The name *Lan Ebdril* (c745)[317] occurs in the Book of Llandaff. But this is listed with churches in Erging and is the old name of Madley in Herefordshire[318, 319].

SO 431170

Llanfaenor (Llanfannar)

lann uannar de machumur (c970)[320], *Sancto Menoro* (1254)[51], *Lanvannar* (1257)[321], *lanvannaro chappell* (1622)[322], *Lanvannor* (1637-8)[323].

Llanfaenor is now the name of a farm which lies approximately 3 miles SE of Skenfrith. But it was the site of an ancient church; a barn between Llanfaenor and Maerdy is 'Chapel Farm' and this may mark the site.

The earliest name-form is from W *llan* 'church' and the p.n. *Banugar* (there is a reference in the Llandaff Charters[324] to *Banugar sacerdos* or 'priest'.

But the name of St. Malo has been added, for *Machumur* is *Machu Mawr* or 'St. Malo the Great'. The neighbouring church of St. Maughans is similarly dedicated to St. Malo[325].

SO 361201

Llangattock Lingoed (Llangatwg Lingoed)

Lancadok (1254)[113], *Lankadduc* (1256-7)[326], *Linchoit*[327], *Landkaddock Kellenny* (c1291)[6], *ecclesia de Lancaddoc Kelleny* (c1348)[5], *Llan Cattoge Iuxta Lyncoyd* (1434)[328], *Langattoke Llyngoed* (1524)[329], *Langattok celenyg* (1577)[8], *Llangattock Kelenig* (1763)[330], *Langattock Lingoed* (1787)[131].

This village is approximately 6 miles NE of Abergavenny. The name has come from the church, i.e. from W *llan* 'church' and the p.n. *Cadoc (Cadwg)*, a famous Welsh saint, so 'Church of Cadoc'.

There are a number of Welsh churches dedicated to St. Cadoc, so each has a further descriptive element as a distinguishing feature.

The present name has Lingoed, a name taken from Llyngoed, once a nearby grange belonging to Dore Abbey. The name-forms here fall into two categories: those with the Lingoed suffix and those with Celenyg; in this latter case the derivation is clearly from W *celyn* 'holly trees' (*celenyg* is an adjective meaning 'abounding in holly trees').

Although, at first sight, Llyngoed appears to have come from W *llyn* 'lake' and W *coed* = *goed* 'wood', this seems inappropriate. There is no sign of a lake hereabouts, and the suspicion arises that *llyn* is an abbreviation of *celyn*. If so, *celynnig* and *(ce)lyn(n)goed* mean the same thing, i.e. 'holly wood' so 'Church of St. Cadoc (near the) holly wood'.

SO 457157

Llangattock Vibion Avel (Llangatwg Feibion Afel)

St. Cadoc (1185)[126], *Lancaddoc* (1230-40)[331], *Linedoc Avel* (1254)[51], *Landcaddock Canel* (c1291)[6], *ecclesia de Lancaddoc auel* (1348)[5], *Lancaddoc Avell* (1455-6)[332], *ll gattwc mibon afel* (c1566)[28], *Llangattock Vibonauel* (1577)[8].

This hamlet lies approximately 2 miles W of Rockfield nr. Monmouth. The name is that of the church, i.e. from W *llan* 'church' and the p.n. *Cadoc (Cadwg)*, so 'Church of St. Cadoc'. Vibion Avel is from W *meibion* = *feibion* 'sons' and the W p.n. *Afel* (Abel), so 'Church of St. Cadoc of the sons of Abel'.

The benefice of a church or estate was received by the impropriator, in this case *Afel (Abel)* and was later passed on by inheritance to his sons and their descendants. In early nameforms 'sons of' i.e. 'vibion' is omitted.

St. Brynach had quite a famous servant, a cattle-drover called Afel[333]; this is a possible source of the name.

SO 397006

Llangeview (Llangyfiw)

Llangevyw (1464)[334], *Llangeview* (1467)[335] (1543)[336] (1765)[23], *Llangevew* (1570)[17].

The hamlet of Llangeview is approximately 1 mile E of Usk town, across the River Usk. The name is from the church i.e. from W *llan* 'church' and the p.n. *Cyfyw,* so 'Church of St. Cyfyw'.

Cyfyw[340] was one of the sons of *Gwynllyw*, first ruler of Gwynllwg (West Gwent). His name occurs in several places in the Llandaff Charters, e.g. *villam lanngatgualitir cum ecclesia sancti Ciuiu* in the Papal Bulls of 1119[34],1128[35] and 1129[36]. But here *ecclesia sancti Ciuiu* 'the Church of St. Cyfyw' is linked with *villam langatgualitir* 'Cadwaladr's estate' which is near Bishton![337]

The explanation appears to be that there were two churches dedicated to St. Cyfyw hereabouts, one at Llangeview Nr. Usk, and the other 'between Caerleon and Caerwent'[338]. It is of interest that the Book of Llandaff refers to a *Dou Civiw* in the parish of Kemeys.[339]

SO 456055

Llangovan (Llangofen)

lanchouian (1193-1218)[342], *Lancomen* (1254)[495], *Llangoven* (1465)[343], *ll y gofain* (c1566)[9], *Llangoven* (1571)[343].

This hamlet is approximately 3 miles SE of Raglan. The name has come from the church, i.e. from W *llan* 'church' and the p.n. *Cwyfen*[345], so 'Church of St. Cwyfen'. This then became 'Church of St. Govan.'

SO 390258

Llangua (Llangiwa)

Languian (1148-83)[346], *Langivay* (1191-98)[349], *Languwan* (1245-53)[347], *Lagywan* (1254)[113], *Llangua* (1330)[348], *Langywan* (c1348)[5], *Llangewa* (1535)[38], *Langua* (1577)[8](1614)[350].

The village of Llangua lies on the N border of Gwent with Herefordshire, near Pontrilas.

The Great House may mark the site of a Benedictine Priory. The name, which is from the church, is from W *llan* 'church' and the p.n. *Ciwa,* so 'Church of St. Ciwa'. Ciwa[351] was an Irish saint.

ST454998

Llangunnog (Llangynog)

henlenic cinauc ar pill (c1005)[352], *Lancannock* (1295)[14], *Lucennouke* (1314)[136], *Llankanynoke* (1488)[353], *Langunnocke* (1712)[354], *Llangunnock (in ruins)* (1836)[212].

Now the name of a farm on the N bank of the Pill Brook, approximately 3 miles E of Llangwm, this was originally the name of an ancient church (reportedly in ruins in 1836).

The earliest name-form is from W *hen* 'old' and W *lennig* diminutive of W *llan* 'church'[355], 'little church', and the p.n. *Cinuac (Cynog = Gynog)* so 'the old small church of Cynog'.

The modern name Llangunnog is thus 'Church of St. Cynog'. Cynog[356] was the eldest son of Brychan, King of Brycheiniog. The ruins of this church are reported to be near the farmhouse known as *Llys Brychan* ('Brychan's Court').

ST 425999

Llangwm (Llan-gwm)

Lan Cum (c860)[357], *lanncum* (c1075)[358], *uillam lann cum cum ecclesiis* (1128)[35] (1129)[36], *Lancum superior* (1254)[495], *Landcom* (c1291)[6], *Lancomb* (1295)[14], *Llangom* (1570)[17], *Langwm* (1806)[360].

This village is some 4 miles E of Usk on the road to Shirenewton and Chepstow (B4235); it is situated in the valley of a tributary of the Olway Brook. The name has come from an original church which was a Celtic Monastic foundation, dedicated to the four Welsh Saints Mingint, Cinficc, Huui and Fruen[71] (in the original spelling). It has come from the position of the church of Llangwm uchaf i.e. from W *llan* 'church' and W *cwm* = *gwm* 'valley' i.e. 'the church in the valley'.

The parish was split into two hamlets (Llangwm-isaf and Llangwm-uchaf 'upper' and 'lower' Llangwm); each had a church. The name Llangwm is found elsewhere in Wales (e.g. near Bala in North Wales).

SO 433007

Llangwm Isaf (Llan-gwm Isaf)

Villa Gunhvcc In Guartha Cum, guarthafcum[358], *[L]angome yssa alias (gwr)da baigh* (after 1601)[361], *parochia de llangome isha* (1555)[150], *Langome yssha* (1604?)[362], *Manor of Llangwm and Gwarda bach*[363](1630-1725).

Once a separate hamlet, further down the valley than Llangwm, hence Llangwm - isaf (from W *isaf* 'lower'). It was also known as Warth-y-cwm; this seems odd at first sight since the derivation is from W *gwarthaf* 'top' or 'utmost point' i.e. 'top of the valley'! In fact, the place was lower down the valley than the other

Llangwm. But in the second and fifth name-forms listed above we find *gwartha bach* i.e. 'top of the little (or side) valley' - not the main valley. This is accurate, topographically.

SO 474032

Llanishen (Llanisien)

lann nissien (c970)[364], *ecclesiam Sancti Dionisii Lannissan* (1223)[365], *Lannissen* (1254)[277], *Lanissen* (c1291)[6], *ecclesia de Lanyssan* (c1348)[106], *Lannyssen, Llanyssen* (1399)[366], *Lannyssen* (c1610)[27], *Llanissen* (1636)[367].

This village is approximately 3 miles N of Devauden on the road to Monmouth (B4293). The name has come from the church, i.e. from W *llan* 'church' and the W p.n. *Isan* or *Isien*[368] (the latter is pronounced 'Ishen') so 'Church of St. Isien.'

The name is found elsewhere e.g. Llanishen near Cardiff.

ST 392986

Llanllowell

Lanluuayl (1155-83)[369], *Landlovel* (1254)[277], *ecclesia de Lanlouel* (c1348)[106], *Llanllowell* (1535)[38], *Llanllowell* (c1610)[27].

The hamlet of Llanllowell lies on the E bank of the river Usk, some two miles below the town of Usk. The name has come from the church i.e. from W *llan* 'church' and the p.n. *Llywel*[370], a form of *Lougil* so 'church of Saint Llywel'. Llywel was a companion of St. Teilo.

Llywel is also the name of a church and hamlet near Trecastle in Powys and there is a Lanlouel near Pleyben in Brittany.

SO 416179

Llanllwyd (Llanlwyd)

ecclesiae Machumur uidelicet Lann Liuit (c970)[371], *St. Liwite of Landiwit* (1186)[126], *Llandlwit* (1230-40)[331], *llanllywid* (1485)[372], *Llanluyth Greene* (1612)[373], *Llanlewith or Llanllewidd* (c1700)[374].

This is now the name of a farmhouse two miles SE of Cross Ash on the Skenfrith to Abergavenny road and near Llanfaenor. But the name was that of an ancient church, the precise location of which is unknown.

This church was *ecclesia Machumur* from L *ecclesia* 'church' and *Machu Mawr* 'St. Malo the Great'[375] so 'Church of St. Malo the Great'. Then the dedication appears to have been changed to that of an obscure saint called *Liwite* so the name became 'Church of St. Liwite'.

Over the years the name Liwite has become W *llwyd* = *lwyd.* This normally means 'grey' or 'pale' though sometimes it appears to be associated with the supernatural.

ST 394894

Llanmartin

lannmarthin (1066-89)[376], *aecclae st. Martini* (1086)[72], *Lanmartin* (1254)[347], *ecclesia de Lanmartyn* (c1348)[238], *ll fartin* (c1566)[28], *Lamnerten* (c1610)[27], *Lanmartin* (1695)[378].

This village lies to the E of Newport, on the road to Magor. The name which has come from the church is from W *llan* 'church' and the p.n. *Martin* i.e. 'Church of St. Martin'. Nothing seems to be known about this saint.

Llanmellin

ST 460290

Llanmellin (1587)[379], *Llanmelyn* (1597)[380], *llanmellyn* (1600)[381], *Lanmellyne* (1630)[382], *Llanmellin* (1704)[383].

Now the name of two farms (Great Llanmellin and Lower Llanmellin) approximately one mile NW of Caerwent; also that of a multivallate Silurian hill-fort nearby (Llanmellin Woods), at the entrance to the Cwm (the valley of the Troggy Brook).

At a first glance the origin of this name may seem clear, i.e. from W *llan* 'church' and W *melin* 'mill.' But there are difficulties.

There was once a mill nearby (Lower Mill). But there is no clear evidence that there ever was a church hereabouts. Moreover, since W *llan* is a feminine noun, W *melin* should have become *felin* in the above name-form.

Bradney[380] has proposed a derivation from W *(g) lan* 'bank' i.e. 'riverbank'. But this would give, somewhat curiously, 'the river bank with the mill' or 'the mill on the river bank'; most water mills were, anyway, on or near a river bank! Moreover, since W *glan* is also a feminine noun, this does not dispose of the previous difficulty i.e. that *melin* should have become *felin.* Rees has pointed out[384] that there are references to a *Llandegelli* or *Llan-y-gelli* which was somewhere in the vicinity. He suggests that the site might be near Lower Mill although Bradney produces evidence[385, 386] suggesting that this place was, in fact several miles upstream, near the old Wentwood Mill.

Mention is made in the Llandaff Charters of Llanfihangel Llechryd (from Llanfihangel 'Church of St. Michael' W *llech* 'flat stone' and W *rhyd* 'ford', i.e. 'Church of St. Michael near the ford (paved with) stone' and it has been suggested[387] that this may have been near Llanmellin hill-fort.

But it is very clear, from the bounds mentioned in the land grant[388] that this place was also upstream; it appears to have been in the same locality as Llandegelli, indeed, the two may be identical.

Thus, so far as Llanmellin is concerned, the derivation remains unclear. A major difficulty is that only relatively late forms of the name have yet been discoverd. The old name of the hillfort is unknown.

ST 496966

Llanquilan (Llangwylan)

Lann Culan Lannculan (c872)[389], *Llanquilan* (1831)[390].

Now the name of a farmhouse in Itton parish, W of Rogerstone Grange. But the name appears to have come from an ancient church somewhere in the vicinity, i.e. from W *llan* 'church' and the p.n. *Culan(n)*[391], so 'Culan(n)'s Church.'

Llanquilan has been identified[392] with Cula lann (1119)(1129) and Culalan (1128), names also occurring in the Book of Llandaff. But these are in lists of names of places in Glamorgan and the identification is dubious. Lann Culan has also been identified with Llangua[688].

SO 442024

Llansoy (Llan-soe Llandysoe)

Lann Tyssoi, podum sancti Tisoi (c725)[393], *Lann Tysoi* (1150)[394], *Landesoy* (1254)[495], *Landisoy* (1295)[14], *ecclesia de Landissoy* (c1348)[106], *Llandesoy* (1427)[395], *lansoy* (1464)[396], *Llansoye* (1544)[397](1577)[8], *Lansoy* (1662)[398].

The village of Llansoy lies approximately 5 miles E of Usk, on a minor road. The name is that of the church, i.e. from W *llan* 'church' and the p.n. *Tyssoi,* so 'Church of St. Tyssoi.' Tyssoi was reputedly a disciple of St. Dyfrig[399].

As can be seen from the name-forms, by about the 16th Century the initial syllable of the name *ty* began to be dropped, on the quite incorrect assumption that this was an honorific prefix and not really part of the name.

SO 278288

Llanthony (Llanddewi Nant Honddu)

Lanthoni (1125-7)[219], (1127-31)[236], *Lantoni* (1148-52)[260], *Lanthotheni, Landewi Nanthotheni* (1214)[287], *Lantonia* (1278)[315], *Lanhodeny, Nant honddy* (1536-9)[414].

Llanthony is famous as the site of a ruined Augustinian Priory in the Honddu Valley, approximately 8 miles N of Abergavenny. Giraldus visited the Priory in 1188 and, commenting on the W name *Landewi Nanthotheni* says also that 'the former humble chapel of St. David is adorned with woodland moss and wreathed with ivy'. This chapel became a monastic site though, subsequently, a second site was established near Gloucester (Llanthony Secunda).

In this name (Llanthony) W *llan* 'church' has replaced an earlier W *nant* originally 'valley' (now 'stream'), Nant Hodni (Honddu) having become *Lanhodeny,* then *Llanthony.* The meaning is 'church of (the brook or valley called) Honddu'. This is a shortened form of the original 'Church of St. David in the Honddu Valley'.

SO 399149

Llantilio Crossenny (Llandeilo Gresynni)

Crissinic (c600)[400], *Lann Teiliau Cressinych* (c600)[401], *sancti teiliaui de crisinic* (1128)[35], *sancti Teliawi crissinic* (1129)[36], *lanteylo cresseny* (1193-1218)[342], *ll deilo groes ynyr* (c1566)[28], *Llanteilio cryssenny* (1577)[8].

This village is some 7 miles to the E of Abergavenny on the road to Monmouth (B4233). The name is that of the church, i.e. from W *llan* 'church' and OW *Teiliau*, W *Teilo* = *Deilo* 'Church of St. Teilo.' It is of interest that the modern name Llantilio actually contains OW *Teiliau* - in 'fossilised' form!

The suffix is from W *croes* 'cross' and the p.n. *Ynyr*, a 6th Century King of Gwent, so 'Church of St. Teilo (near the) Cross of Ynyr.'

SO 311163

Llantilio Pertholey (Llandeilo Bertholau)

Lann Maur id est Lann Teiliau porth halauc (c600)[403], *sancti teliaui deporth halauc* (1128)[35], *Llantheill' Porthaleg* (1254)[51], *Llanteylo Perthologǵ* (1442-50)[104], *Llandilobarthole* (1577)[8], *Lantilio Pertholey* (1615)[404].

The village of Llantilio Pertholey lies some 2 miles N of Abergavenny. The name has come from the church i.e. from Llantilio 'Church of St. Teilo' (see preceding entry on Llantilio Crossenny). At first sight the suffix appears to be from W *perth* = *berth* 'bush' 'hedge' or possibly 'wood' and W *olau* 'ancient trackway(s).' But a study of the name-forms demonstrates that the first element is W *porth* 'gate' or 'gateway' (often used of an entrance to a monastic grange).

The second element is less straightforward. It looks like W *halog* though this normally means 'polluted' or 'defiled' and this meaning does not really fit here. It has been pointed out[405] that in Cornish, *hal* (from British **haloc*) originally meant 'dirty water' then 'standing water' then 'marsh.' Assuming the same meaning in Old Welsh, this would give 'gateway on the marshy land,' so 'Church of St. Teilo near the gateway on the marshy land.' The place lies on the Gavenny brook.

It should be noted, however, that *Alauc* is also a p.n.

ST 392969

Llantrisant (Llantrisaint)

ecclesia sancti Petri de Lantrissen (1155-83)[406], *Lantrissan* (1220-1)[407](1314)[136], *Lantrissan* (1248)[408], *Lantrissen* (1295)[14], *ecclesia de Lantrissan* (c1348)[106], (1474)[409], *y trisaint* (c1566)[9], *Lantrissent* (1684)[410], *Lantrisent* (1697)[411], *Llantrisaint* (1845)[412].

The name of this village which is on the E bank of the River Usk, 4 miles S of Usk town, has come from the church which was originally dedicated to the three Welsh saints Dyfrig, Teilo and Euddogwy (Odouceus); the dedication is now to St. Peter, St. Paul and St. John. Hence the derivation from W *llan* 'church', W *tri* 'three' and W *sant* 'saint' (*sant* is actually singular but is here used after *tri* in a plural sense), so 'Church of the Three Saints.'

The name is found elsewhere, e.g. Llantrisant, Glamorgan.

ST 434918

Llanvaches (Llanfaches)

ecclesiam merthirmaches (c755)[413], *Lanmaueis* (1193-1218)[128], *Lanmaes* (1254)[277], *Lamatheys* (c1291)[6], *Lamaghois* (1306)[415], *Lanmaucheys* (c1348)[238], *Lanvaghes* (1567)[416], *Llanuaghes* (c1610)[27], *Lanvaches* (1661)[417].

The village of Llanvaches lies approximately 8 miles to the E of Newport; the name has come from the church. The earliest name is from L *ecclesia* 'church', W *merthyr* (ex L *martyrium*) 'place associated with a martyr' and the p.n. *Maches* = *Faches,* so 'Church of St. Maches.'

Maches[418] was a daughter of Gwynllyw, first ruler of Gwynllwg (now W Gwent).

ST 448924

Llanvair Discoed (Llanfair Isgoed)

Lamecare (1086)[72], *Lanueir* (1193-1218)[128], *Lànnveyr* (1306)[227], *Llanveyre Iskoed* (1535)[38], *ll fair is koed* (c1566)[28], *Llanuaier* (1577)[8], *Lanveyrthies koed* (1585)[161], *Lanvaire Escoide* (1633)[169], *llanvaier dyscoid* (1596)[704], *Lanvayre iscoid* (1640-1)[170], *Llanvaire Discoed* (1711)[207].

This village lies at the foot of Grey Hill (Mynydd Llwyd) between Newport and Chepstow; it has the ruins of a 13th Century castle. The name is from the church i.e. from W *llan* 'church' and the p.n. *Mair* = *Fair* 'Mary', so 'Church of St. Mary.'

The distinguishing suffix *iscoed* (into which an extraneous *d* has been introduced) is from W *is* 'below' and W *coed* 'wood', so 'Church of St. Mary below the Wood.' The wood referred to is, of course, Wentwood.

There is some doubt whether the earliest name-form actually is that of this Llanfair.

SO 367141

Llanvapley (Llanfable)

ecclesiam Mable (c860)[419], *Eglosemapel* (1254)[51], *Llanvapley* (1482)[420], *St. Mabill, Lanvapley* (1540)[421], *ll. vablle* (c1566)[28], *Lanvapley* (1599)[422](c1610)[27].

This is the name of a hamlet and mansion house (Llanvapley Court) approximately 5 miles E of Abergavenny, on the road to Monmouth (B4233). The name has come from the church which is dedicated to St. Mabel; it is from W *llan* 'church' and the W p.n. *Mable = Fable* 'Mabel', so 'Church of St. Mabel'. Earlier forms are from L *ecclesia* 'church' and W *eglwys* 'church.'

Nothing seems to be known about this particular saint[423].

SO 363172

Llanvetherine (Llanwytherin)

Ecclesia Gueithirin (c876)[424], *Linwerthin* (1254)[51], *Lanwetheryn* (c1291)[6], *ecclesia de Lanwytheryn* (c1348)[5], *Llanwytheryn* (1349-53)[425], *Llanvetherin* (1514)[426], *Lanvitherine* (1794)[427].

This village is approximately 6 miles NE of Abergavenny on the road to Skenfrith. The name is that of the church, i.e. from W *llan* 'church' and the p.n. *Gwytherin* 'Church of St. Gwytherin.'

Little is known about Gwytherin[428] the reputed founder of this church. This saint's name occurs elsewhere, e.g. Gwytherin, Denbigh, N Wales.

SO 325207

Llanvihangel Crucorney (Llanfihangel Crucornau)

lann Mihacqel cruc cornou (c970)[429], *Sancti Michaelis de Crukorn* (1254)[113], *Sci Michis Kilcornu* (c1291)[6], *ecclesia sancti Michaelis Kistornew* (c1348)[5], *Llanvihangell Krigcorne* (1444/5)[430], *Michaelchurch Crucorne* (1577)[8], *Llanvihangel Crucorney* (1767)[431].

This is a village some 6 miles N of Abergavenny on the road to Hereford (A465), it is also on the Honddu brook. The name is from the church i.e. from W *llan* 'church' and the W p.n. *Mihangel = Fihangel* 'Michael', so 'Church of St. Michael.'

The first element of the distinguishing suffix *Crucorney (Crucornau)* is W *crûg* 'cairn' or 'mound' but sometimes 'hill'. The second element appears to be W *cornau,* plural of W *corn* 'horn' and, indeed, 'horned hill' has been suggested though this requires explanation.

It is true that, seen from the SW, the nearby Skirrid Mountain appears to have two protuberances atop. But W *corn* may also mean 'point or cairn on a mountain-top[432]. It seems very likely that Crucorney refers to the Skirrid with its irregular, angled shape. Indeed Bradney has made this point. Crugkorny is also a Breton name-form.

SO 347093

Llanvihangel Gobion (Llanfihangel-y-gofion)

Sancti Michaelis iuxta Usk (1254)[51], *Lamyhangel* (c1291)[6], *sancti Michaelis iuxta usk* (c1348)[5], *Lanvihangel-nigh-Usk* (1551-3)[434], *ll. V'el y gofion* (c1566)[28], *Saint Michael, Dyffryn Usk* (1583)[435].

This hamlet, with a church from which the name has come, lies midway between Abergavenny and Raglan, approximately 7 miles N of Usk. The name is from Llanvihangel 'Church of St. Michael' (see previous entry, Llanvihangel Crucorney). The suffix *Gobion* appears to be from a precursor *(*gobannos)* of W *gof* (pl. *gofaint*) 'smith', so 'Church of St. Michael (near the) settlement of (black) smiths'.

ST 452278

Llanvihangel Rogiet (Llanfihangel Rogiet)

Tref Peren id est Lann mihacgel maur (c905)[436], *sanctum Michaelem* (1086)[72], *Lann Mihacgel maur* (1119)[34], *Lanmihangel* (1254)[277](c1291)[6], *Llannehangell* (1577)[8], *Llanfihangel Roggiet* (1598)[437], *Lanvihangel Rogiet* (1636)[438].

This was once the name of a Manor; it is now that of a hamlet near Rogiet. The name has come from the church i.e. from W *llan* 'church' and the p.n. *Mihangel* = *Fihangel* 'Michael' with the name of the nearby village, Rogiet, as a distinguishing suffix, so 'Church of St. Michael (near) Rogiet.'

The original name *Lann Mihacgel Maur* (from W *mawr* 'great') probably means 'Great St. Michael's.'

SO 464018

Llanvihangel Tor-y-Mynydd

ecclesia de lanvihangell kennan, alias dicitur lanihangell tormeneth (late C14)[439], *ll. V'el tor mynyd* (c1566)[28], *Llanvehangel terremenyth* (1577)[8], *Lanvihangle Tourmoneth* (1625)[433], *Llanfihangel Tory Monyth* (1695)[440].

This isolated church, with its own very small parish is approximately 1 mile S of Llanishen; Llanvihangel Court is nearby. The name is from *Llanvihangel (Llanfihangel)* i.e. 'Church of St. Michael' (see previous entry) with the distinguishing suffix *tor-y-mynydd.*

In modern Welsh *tor*, used in this connection, means 'break' or 'gap.' But looking at the topography here, the meaning seems more akin to that of OW *twrr* 'bulge'; *tor-y-mynydd* would then be 'the bulge of the mountain', so 'Church of St. Michael near the bulge of the mountain.' This is a good description of the position of the place, lying below the protruding spur of Star Hill.

Bradney[441] gives 'Church of St. Michael on the breast of the hill.'

SO 432129

Llanvihangel Ystern Llewern (Llanfihangel Ystum Llewern)

Sancti Michaelis (1254)[51], *Eston lowern* (1273), *Lanvyhangel Estelwecon* (c1291)[6], *ecclesia de Estomlowern* (c1348)[5], *St. Michael ystyn llevryn* (1499)[442], *Llanyhangell Istym llewyrn* (1540)[443], *Llanvihangell Isten Lleuwern* (1612)[444], *Llanyhangle* (c1610)[27], *Llanvihangell ystern llewerne* (1767)[445].

This is a village on the River Trothy (Troddi) some 7 miles NW of Monmouth. The name is from that of the church i.e. from *Llanvihangel (Llanfihangel)* 'Church of St. Michael' (see previous entry) with a distinguishing suffix which is either *ystern llewern* or *ystum llewern;* to date the assumption appears to have been made that *ystum* is the correct form and that *ystern* is a corrupt form of this. But this may not be correct. The second element in the suffix, *llewern*, has been interpreted in several different ways. Bradney[690] has suggested a derivation from W *tan llewryn* 'will-o-the wisp,'[447] recounting an obviously apocryphal story of the origin of this. A derivation from W *llewern* 'fox' has also been proposed[448], but, in fact, *Llewern* was probably an OW p.n.[449 450] based on W *llawern* (pl. *llewryn*) 'fox' and with equivalents in Cornish *(lowern)* and Breton *(louarn)*. It is found in place-names such as Llanllower (Llanllowern) in Pembs., and Trelowarren in Brittany. The name is found in the Book of Llandaff e.g. *cruc leuyrn* + *cricou leuirn*.

As indicated previously, it seems to have been generally accepted that *Ystern* has come from W *ystum* 'river bend.' The difficulty is that in this case *ystum* is not really appropriate topographically. The course of the River Trothy (Troddi) is sinuous, but without major bends (though river courses may change over the years). But a possibility needing to be considered is that *ystern* may have come from W *estyn* or *ystyn* meaning 'gift' or 'present'[446 451]. If so, the meaning of the place-name becomes 'The Church of St. Michael (on or near the) land granted (or possessed) by Llewyrn.' This appears to make more sense than the other derivations suggested.

SO 277148

Llanwenarth

Sancto Waynardo (1254)[51], *Lanwaynard* (c1291)[6], *Lanwenarth* (1538-44)[535], *Lanwenarth* (1542-3)[541], *Lanwennarth* (1707)[555].

This church and hamlet lies approximately 2 miles W of Abergavenny, near the banks of the River Usk. The name is from W *llan* 'church' and the p.n. *Gwenarth (Guainerth),* a saint's name found in the Book of Llandaff[709]. Under mutation, *Gwenarth* has become *Wenarth.* The meaning of the name is thus 'Gwenarth's Church.' Gwenarth is also the patron saint of St. Weonards (Llansainwenarth) in Herefordshire.

ST 371879

Llanwern (Llan-wern)

Lanwarin (1254)[347](1319-22)[452], *Lannarein* (c1291)[6], *Lanwaryn* (1321-2)[453](c1348)[238], *ll, wern* (c1566)[28], *Llanwern* (1509-47) [454], *Llanwarn* (1577)[8], *Llanwarne* (1597)[455], *Lanwern* (c1790)[135].

This village, to the E of Newport was once in a rural area, but is now in close proximity to the Spencer Steelworks. The name is from the church, i.e. from W *llan* 'church' and W *(g)wern* 'alder trees' synonymous with 'swamp', so 'Church (in or near) the alder swamp.'

In the above name-forms W *gwern* seems to have been anglicised quite early on; *lannguern timauc* mentioned in the Book of Llandaff (c970)[703] may refer to Llanwern. In the same way the earliest form of the name of Llanwarne Court, Herefordshire seems to have been Lannguern (c758)[456]; it has become Llanwarne.

SO 464048

Llanwinney

Llanwini (1570)[16].

This is now the name of a farm in the parish of Llangovan, approximately 2 miles N of Llanishen. The name is that of an ancient chapel, once hereabouts, dedicated to St. Gwenny, a form of *Winwaloe*[457]. The name is from W *llan* 'church' and this p.n. *(G)wenny,* so 'Church of St. Gwenny.'

Magor (Magwyr)

ST 870425

Magor (1153-76)[705](1234-40)[458](1254)[347](1536)[459](1577)[8], *ecclesia de Magor* (c1348)[238], *Magwyr* (1568)[460].

This is a large village approximately 6 miles to the E of Newport, on the road to Caldicot. The name is from W *magwyr* (ex L *maceria* 'wall') 'walls' or 'enclosure' (used of ruins).

The name also occurs in Cornwall and, significantly, the place so-named is the site of the only Roman villa in Cornwall[461].

Maindee (Maendy)

ST 325885

The Maendy (1615)[462], *Mayndee House* (1674)[463], *Mayndee bach farm* (1787)[464], *Mayndee Vawr Farm* (1787)[465], *Maindee* (1803)[466].

Now the name of an eastern suburb of Newport, this is from W *maen* 'stone' and W *tŷ = dy* 'house' i.e. 'the stone house.' In this case the name appears to refer to a mansion house in Eveswell. But the name is found elsewhere in Wales. It is found in the 12th Century Llandaff Charters.

Mardy (Maerdy)

SO 307157

Merdiu (1256-7)[148].

This name-form is for Mardy near Abergavenny though the name is found widely in Wales, often in the form *Maerdy* which is from W *maer* 'steward' and W *ty* 'house' i.e. 'the steward's house.'

The *Maer* was the chief officer (bailiff) of a commote in pre-Norman times and the Maerdy was on the commotal demesne. By association with the above, Maerdy may sometimes also mean 'dairy farm'[149].

ST 523909

Mathern (Matharn)

merthir teudiric (c900)[467], *Villam Merthir Teudiric cum ecclesiis* (1119)[34], *uillam mertyr teudiric* (1128)[35], *Ecclesia de Martharne* (1193-1218 or 1254)[468], *Martherne* (1245-53)[469](1361)[227](1640)[470], *Matharne* (c1610)[27].

Mathern is a village about 1 mile SW of Chepstow with a 15th Century building used as a palace by the Bishops of Llandaff from 1406 to 1706.

The name Mathern is associated primarily with that of Tewdrig ap Teithfallt, King of Gwent and Glamorgan in the 6th Century. He had retired but was called back to fight a successful battle against the Saxons near Tintern[471]. He was killed but was buried at Mathern where his son Meurig founded a church in memory of him.

The earliest name-form is thus from W *merthyr* (ex L *martyrium*) 'place where a martyr is commemorated' or 'church', and the p.n. *Tewdrig,* so 'church where Tewdrig is commemorated.' In later forms *merthyr* has become *Marther* (as for instance, in nearby Marthergeryn) and a terminal *n* has been acquired. The name has been shortened.

The suggestion has been made that the derivation is from W *ma* 'place' and W *teyrn* 'King' i.e. 'the King's place'[472]. But this does not fit the name-forms.

Milton

ST 367884

Meleton (c1291)[468], *Salesbury and Multon* (1314)[136], *Multon* (1319)[473], *Mylton* (1597)[474], *Milton* (1598)[475].

This hamlet is near Llanwern, to the E of Newport. The name, found quite frequently in England and Wales, is derived from the mill which was once here, i.e. from OE *mylen* 'mill' and OE *tun (-ton)* 'farm' or 'estate' then, later 'settlement' (then 'town'), so 'farm or settlement near the mill.' The Welsh equivalent is Felindre from W *melin* = *felin* and W *tre(f)* = *dre.*

Mitchell Troy (Llanfihangel Troddi)

SO 492103

Mychell Troie (1551-2)[476]. *ll. V'el trodi* (c1566)[28], *Michel troy* (c1610)[27].

This village is approximately 2 miles S of Monmouth on the River Trothy (Troddi); Troy House is about a mile away to the E. The name Troy has come from that of the River *Tro(dd)i* and *Mitchell* is OE *micel* 'great', used to distinguish the place from the hamlet downstream (*) (*Troy parva* or "*litell-Troye*")[477].

The Welsh form *Llanfihangel Troddi* may well have arisen because Mitchell has been confused with the name Michael (W *Mihangel* = *Fihangel*).

(*) as in the case of Mitchel dean, Gloucestershire[478].

SO 510130

Monmouth (Trefynwy)

Blestium (C3)[479], *aper myngui* (c733)[480], *aper Mynuy* (c733)[481], *castellum de mingui* (1066-89)[482], *Monemude* (1086)[483], *Monemuta* (1254)[484], *Munmuth* (1265)[485], *Monemuth* (1341)[486], *Monemouth* (1429)[487], *tre fynwe* (c1566)[9], *Monmouth* (1577)[8].

This town, once the County Town of Monmouthshire (which took its name from the town), lies on the NE border of Gwent, at the confluence of the Monnow (Mynwy) and the Wye. Both rivers are crossed by stone bridges, that over the Monnow (Mynwy) having a celebrated 14th/15th Century gatehouse. There are the ruins of a castle and there was once a Benedictine Priory here. The Grammar School dates from 1615.

The earliest name-form *Blestium* (or *Blestio*) was that of a Romano-British settlement here; the name has probably come from a Gaulish p.n.[479]. The next name-form is from OW and W *aber* 'mouth of river' and the river name *Mynwy* (the tributary flowing into the Wye). Then *aber* is replaced by OE *mupa = muta* 'mouth' and finally this has become E *mouth*. All forms mean 'Mouth of the Monnow' (or Mynwy)[488]; they describe the geographical location of the town.

The W form Trefynwy is from W *tre* originally 'farm' or 'estate' then 'settlement,' and the name of the river, so 'settlement on the Mynwy.'

ST 512931

Mounton

uillam Guennonoe (c730)[489], *Villa Gvinnonvi* (c730)[490], *Monketowne* (1535)[38], *Mounton chap.* (1577)[8], *Monckton* (1613)[491], *Mounton* (1613)[492].

This village which lies approximately 1½ miles W of Chepstow was once a possession of Chepstow Priory. The name is, accordingly, from E *monk* and OE *tun (-ton)* 'farm' or 'estate', i.e. 'the monks' estate.'

The earliest name-form is from L *villa* 'estate' and the p.n. *Guinnonui* (Gwenonwy). Gwenonwy was the daughter of Meurig ab Tewdrig, King of Gwent in the 6th Century.

The name is found elsewhere, e.g. Mounton, Pembs[493].

ST 520909

Moyne's Court

Moyne's Court (1543)[494], *Moynescowrte* (1567)[174], *Moyne's Court (and Barrons Greene)* (1682)[496].

This is a many gabled 16th or early 17th Century mansion with a turreted gatehouse to the W of Mathern; the house was built on the site of an earlier castle. The name is that of the one-time owners, the de Moigne family.

SO 525065

The Narth

waste land called the Narth (1612-82)[647].

This village lies some 2 miles to the N of Trelleck. The name appears to have come from W *garth* 'enclosure' i.e. *yn arth* ('soft' mutation with loss of definite article) 'in the enclosure.'

ST 345837

Nash (Trefonen)

capella de Fraxino (1289)[497], *Fraxinum* (1290)[498], *Assh* (1322)[497], *Asshe* (1334)[497], (1393-4)[90], *ecclesia de ffraxino* (c1348)[238], *Nasch* (1535)[38], *Nashe* (1577)[8].

The village of Nash lies near the mouth of the River Usk and on the E bank; it was once a possession of Goldcliff Priory.

The earliest name-forms are from L *fraxinus* 'ash tree', later forms from OE *aesc* also 'ash tree'. The *n* in Nash seems to have come from ME *atten* 'at' so the name really means 'at the ash tree'[497].

The name is found elsewhere, e.g. Nash Manor nr Llysworney, Glamorgan, and Nash Farm in Herefordshire (Asshe, 1307; Nash, 1355)[499]. It is also found at Nash Point in Glamorgan and the question arising is whether a derivation from OE *naess* 'cape' or 'headland' may be appropriate here. But the name appears to have come from nearby Monknash (derived in the same way as Nash Manor and Nash nr. Newport). Ekwall has pointed out that OE *naess* becomes *nes(s)*.

ST 453976

Newchurch (Eglwys Newydd ar y Cefn)

Newchurche, Newchurch (1509)[500], *Newchurche* (1535)[501] (1567)[502] *yr eglwys newydd ar y kefen* (c1566)[9].

This village of widely dispersed houses and farms lies between Usk and Chepstow; the church has a very large parish. The name has come from this church which is attributed to the monks of

Tintern who began building it in the 12th century (hence the name 'new' church).

The W name *Eglwys Newydd ar y Cefn* means 'the new church on the ridge.'

SO 502141

Osbaston

Villa Osberti (c1070)[503], *Hosebuston* (1274)[503], *Osbertston* (1345)[503], *Osberston* (1460-1)[504].

This small village, once with iron and tinplate works, lies immediately N of Monmouth.

The earliest name-form is from L villa *'estate'* or 'farm'; later name-forms are from OE *tun* (-ton) meaning the same thing. The other element here is the p.n. *Osbert,* derived from the OE p.n. *Osbeorht,* so 'Osbert's farm or estate'[503].

ST 408917

Parc Seymour

Park Seymor (1567)[154].

Now a housing development on the N side of the A48 road, approximately 1 mile W of Penhow; the old name of nearby land has been retained.

The name is from W *parc* 'park' and the family name *Seymour (St. Maur).* The Seymours held Penhow and the Manor of Castell Coch[708].

SO 522094

Penallt

Pennald (1295)[14], *Penalthe* (1314)[136], *Pennalth* (c1348)[106], *pen allt* (c1566)[9], *Pennalth* (c1610)[27].

This village is in a secluded position above the cliffs of the Wye Valley (west bank) and approximately 2½ miles to the S of Monmouth.

The name is from W *pen* 'head' or 'top' and W *gallt* = *allt* 'cliff' or 'slope' (often 'wooded slope' in S. Wales), so 'on the top of the cliffs or wooded slope.'

The name reflects the topographical position of the place, especially as seen from Monmouth.

SO 452079

Penclawdd (Pen-y-clawdd)

Penetlan (1254)[277], *Penchland* (1295)[14], *Penclath* (1342)[505], *ecclesia de Penclaw* (c1348)[106], *Penclawth* (1442)[506], *Penclawthe* (1499)[507].

This hamlet lies approximately 4 miles E of Raglan, on a minor road.

The name is from W *pen* 'head' or 'end' (in this case the latter) and W *clawdd* 'dyke' or 'ditch' also 'fence', 'wall' or 'hedge' so '(at the) end of the dyke or ditch'.

Bradney[508] says that the name has been taken from the earthworks on which the church stands. In fact, the church stands at the end of a ditch which probably marked a boundary of some antiquity[712].

ST 407895

Pencoed

Pencoyde (1270)[575], *Pencoyd* (1542)[510].

This is a moated mansion house with parts dating back to the thirteenth century, situated on the site of a Norman castle, some 2 miles N of Magor. The original owners were a family called de la More, but the place was rebuilt in the 16th Century by a member of the Morgan family.

The name is from W *pen* 'head' or 'end' (in this case the latter) and W *coed* 'wood' so '(at the) end of the wood.' The wood referred to is, of course, Wentwood.

The name is found elsewhere in Wales, e.g. Pencoed nr. Bridgend.

ST 425908

Penhow

Penhou (1130-39)[511], *Pennho, Pentilio* (1193-1218)[128], *Penho* (1254)[347](c1291)[6], *Penhow* (1306)[513], *Penho* (1361)[227], *pen hw* (c1566)[28], *Penhow* (c1610)[27].

Now the name of a village about five miles E of Newport, this was originally that of the nearby small castle and church built on the end of a ridge overlooking the Newport to Chepstow road (A48). The castle was reputedly built by Sir William de Sancto Mauro (St. Maur or Seymour, hence nearby Parc Seymour).

The name is a hybrid, from W *pen* 'end' (in this case) and OE *hoh* 'projecting ridge', so 'end of the ridge.' This is a topographically accurate description of the position of the castle.

The form *Pentilio* (1193-1218) appears to have come from W *pen* and *tilio* or *teliau;* this appears to have come from W *(a) deiliau*[713] (plural of W *adail*) 'buildings', so 'head' or 'end' or 'height' with buildings.'

SO 416117

Penrhos (Pen-rhôs)

Panrox (1186)[515], *Caddoci de penros* (1193-1218)[516], *Penros* (1254)[51](1256-7)[517], *Ponres* (c1291)[6], *Lancaddoc Penros* (c1348)[106], *Penrose* (1531)[518](1588)[519], *Pen Ros* (c1566)[28], *Penrhos* (1588)[514].

This is a village with a church with a large parish and with houses widely dispersed, some three miles N of Raglan. It is also the name of a place near Caerleon (*Penrose-juxta Carylon* (1651/2))[520].

The name is from W *pen* 'head' or 'end' and W *rhos.* This latter word usually means 'moorland'. But in the Cornish language it means 'hill-spur' or 'promontory'[693] and this would make much more sense in the present case(s), so 'end of the hill-spur.'

The name Penrose is found in Cornwall[693].

ST 522998

Penterry

Territorium lann bedeui (955)[521], *lann Vedeui* (955)[522], *Pentir* (1231-4)[523], *Pentir, Pentiry* (1223)[524], *Penterry, Pentirrie* (1587)[525], *Pentire* (1597)[526], *Pentiri* (1605)[527], *Penterye Chap.* (c1610)[27].

This is now the name of a farm and that of a church with a small parish in an isolated situation. It was once a hamlet and is also an ancient ecclesiastical site.

The original name is from W *llan* 'church' and, probably, the p.n. *Medwy* (*) = *Fedwy*[528], i.e. 'Medwy's Church.' But there has then been a complete change of name.

Earlier new name-forms: *Pentir* (1148-76) and *Pentir, Pentiry* (1223) suggest a derivation from W *pentir* 'headland'; this has then acquired a terminal *y*. Looking at the geography of the area, this derivation would be appropriate.

Pentire in Cornwall has come from Corn. *pen-tyr* 'headland'[529].

(*) though a derivation from W *bedw* 'birch trees' may also be possible; there is a Coed Vedw nearby.

ST 524981

Porthcasseg

agrum porthcassec (c693)[533], *villa de Porcassek* (1223)[534], *Port Kassach* (1230-40)[458], *Port asse* (c1291)[6], *ecclesia de Porth casseg* (c1348)[238], *Port Cassegg* (1717)[536].

This is the name of a farm and hamlet 1 mile N of St. Arvans. There was once an ancient settlement here and, later on, this was a grange or monastic farm belonging to Tintern Abbey. There was also an ancient church here and on the farm, itself, is a building which may have been used as a chapel.

As it stands, the name appears to be from W porth *'gate'* or 'gateway' and W *caseg* 'mare', i.e. 'the mare's gateway' (although, frankly, this does not appear to make much sense and one suspects a more profound, underlying meaning).

ST 352977

Porth llong

Porth-y-llong (1688)[589].

Name of a farmhouse on a minor road from Llangibby to Coed-y-paen village, approximately 2 miles from each. The word *llong* means 'ship' in modern Welsh, but in place names containing this word a derivation from W *llwng* 'damp' or 'marshy' has been suggested[590].

However, the topography of this place, in itself, suggests a different derivation. Porth llong farmhouse stands near a narrow gap through which a minor road passes and upon which two other minor roads converge. It is thus near a narrow aperture or 'gullet' (W *llwnch*) and it seems likely that *(l)long* has in fact come from this word. Quite nearby, the name *Pwll-y-llwnch* is found on the river Usk (below Llangibby); this is a place where the river narrows at a bend.

The derivation from W *porth* 'gate' + W *llwnch* (in this sense) 'narrow entrance' or 'defile' is thus 'gate of the defile'.

ST 383833

Porton

Portreuestun (1245)[408], *Portreveston* (1307, 1348)[694], *Porterton* (1388)[532], *Portertone* (1398)[695], *Porton* (1598)[531].

This place, near Goldcliff, was once an Anglo-Norman settlement, with a church (now gone).

The earliest name-form is from OE *portreeve* 'chief officer of a borough' (after the Norman Conquest), and OE *tun (-ton)* 'farm' or 'estate', i.e. 'the Portreeve's estate.' Portreveston has then been contracted to Porton. This name, formed in the same way, is found elsewhere, e.g. Porton Down, Wiltshire.

ST 505883

Portskewett (Porth Sgiwed, Porth Ysgewin)

Portascibth (1065)[540], *Poteschiuet* (1086)[72], *porth isceuin* (1128)[35] (1129)[36], *Portesc(hiwet)* (1190)[542], *Porth scuwet* (1245-53)[74], *Porteskywet* (c1291)[6], *Portscuwet* (c1348)[543], *Porteskewet* (c1610)[27], *Portescuet* (1789)[544], *Portskewett* (1796)[545].

This village which is not far from the seacoast is some 4 miles to the W of Chepstow, on the road from Caldicot.

In the Welsh Triads[546] (Trioedd Ynys Prydein) *Porth Ys(g)ewin* (c1150) was reputed to be 'one of the three principal harbours of Britain' though the actual site (St. Pierre Pill?) is not known and Portskewett is now an inland village. But this previous activity is clearly reflected in the name, the first element of which is W *porth* 'harbour' (in this case).

Now the last element may be *cuit*[548], an old form of *coed* 'wood' more usually found in the Cornish language[547] (though coit is both a Welsh and Cornish form). If so, then the second element is 'below', so 'harbour below the wood', the wood being Wentwood (or *coit gwent*[549]). The place seems at one time to have been the principal harbour of Gwent Iscoed.

Some forms, particularly the older W ones have *isceuin* or *ys(g)ewin* as an element and this has been interpreted as W *ysgawen* 'elder trees'[550]. But there may also be echoes here of the W p.n. *Isgawyn.*

ST 519925

Pwllmeyric

pull mouric (c625)[553], *aper pull Muric* (c620)[551], *aper muric* (c620)[552], *Poulmeweryk* (1306)[554], *ecclesia de Pulmeuric* (c1348) [232], *Polmerck* (1393-4)[556], *Polemerigg* (1711)[557].

The village of Pwllmeyric lies to the W of Chepstow. The name has come from a pool in the little river running through, which at one time took its name from the pool; it is now called the Mounton brook.

The name Pwllmeyric is from W *pwll* 'pool' or 'well' and the p.n. *Meurig* i.e. 'Meurig's Pool.' Meurig was a King of Gwent, son of Tewdrig (see Mathern).

Now W *pwll* i.e. pill may also mean 'estuarine inlet' e.g. Mathern Pill, Caldicot Pill etc. But it is clear that *pwll* is not used in this sense in the present name.

For instance, in the Llandaff Charters we read of *vallem putei maurit* i.e. 'the valley of the pool or well of Meurig' and of going from *'Aber pwll Meurig'* (i.e. the place where the Pwllmeurig brook enters the sea) up the river 'to the *pwll*'[558]. At one time the Pwllmeurig brook was known simply as the *Mouric (Meurig)*[559].

Bradney[560] reports that 'the well' is on the W side of the road leading to Mathern.

Pye-Corner

Pye Corner (Christchurch) (1704)[537].

This rather odd name is found both to the W of Newport (in Bassaleg) and to the E (in Nash). It is found in Chepstow and elsewhere.

The name, which appears to be somewhat facetious, has probably come from the surname Pie or Pye; both forms are recorded in Gwent in the early 1400s[538, 702]. Pye Corner in Gloucestershire is said to have taken its name from a Richard de la Pey (1248)[539].

SO 412077

Raglan

Raglam (c1090)[652], *villa Ragthan* (1174)[561], *Raghelan* (1254)[495], *Ragelan* (c1291)[6], *Raglan* (1314)[136], *Ragelan* (c1348)[106], *Ragland* (1577)[8].

The small town of Raglan, between Usk and Monmouth, has an imposing ruined 'castle' (actually the mansion of the Marquis of Worcester, dating from the 15th Century).

Richards[562] gives a derivation of the name from W *rhag* 'front' or 'fore' and W *(g)lan* 'bank' (this is supposedly used here in the sense of 'fortification') to give 'forward fortification.' However, name-forms preceded by L *villa* are not infrequently followed by the name of the owner or occupier of the 'estate'; in *villa Ragthan* (1174) we have an example of this type so that *'Ragthan' (Ragllan?)* may well be a p.n. (c.f. Baglan).

Bradney[563] gives the derivation 'front bank'; this is said to suggest that Raglan was 'a place of exceptional prospect and views.' In fact, this is a rather undulating landscape (though, of course, the views are pleasant). But this derivation seems unlikely.

ST 412842

Redwick

Redewic (1290)[564], *Redwik(e)* (1313)[564], *Radewyk(e)* (1317) (1397) (1411) (1413)[564], *Rodewyk* (1319)[565], *Redewik* (1477)[566], *Reddwicke* (1535)[38], *Yr Redwic* (c1566)[565, 28].

This village lies E of Goldcliff, near the sea-coast. Redwick appears have been the site of an early Anglo-Norman settlement. The field-names appear, originally, to have been English, it is said that by the 18th Century most had become Welsh.

The name also occurs in England, e.g. Redwick, Gloucestershire, and this name has been derived from OE *hread* 'reeds' and OE *wic* (ex L *vicus*) 'farm' or 'hamlet', so 'the farm in the reeds'[567] and in view of the location this would seem to have been appropriate. But Charles[564] has pointed out that in this case the name-forms with *rade,* possibly from OE *read* 'red', may point to 'the red farm.'

S0 482149

Rockfield

lann guoronoi (c970)[568], *Lannguronoi* (c1020)[569], *ecclesia de Rochevilla* (c1069) (1164)[570], *Rokeuile* (1193-1218)[571], *ecclesia de Rokeuille* (1199)[570], *Rochevill, ch. of St. Guerialoc* (1230-40)[331], *Roukevile* (c1291)[6], *ecclesia de Rokeuylo*(c1348)[5], *Rokefeld* (c1610)[27], *Rockfield* (1763)[170].

The village of Rockfield lies some 2 miles NE of Monmouth. The first name (now lost) was that of a very early church hereabouts, i.e. from W *llan* and the p.n. *Guoronoi* (Goronwy), so 'Goronwy's Church.'

But after the Norman Conquest, the place was renamed after Rocheville in France; this has come from Fr. *roche* 'rock or stone' and Fr. *ville* now 'town' but originally 'estate'. The name has been Anglicised, *roche* has become 'rock' and *ville* 'field'.

Rogerstone Grange

ST 506966

grangia de Rogereston (1222)[572](1307)[572], *Rogenston* (c1291)[509] (1234-40)[458], *grangia de Rogeston* (1535)[572], *The grange* (1577)[8].

Once a grange or monastic farm belonging to Tintern Abbey, but now the name of a farm (once the Home Farm for the Curre family).

The name is from the p.n. *Roger*[573] (Roger de Clare, Earl of Hertford and nephew of Walter de Clare, founder of Tintern Abbey; his son was also named Roger), and OE *tun (-ton)* 'farm' or 'estate' i.e. 'Roger's estate.'

There is another Rogerstone near Newport, in W Gwent, but this is named after Roger de Berkerolles[574].

Rogiet

ST 462878

Rogiet (1193-1218)[128], *Roge(r)ate* (1245-53)[347], *Rogwate* (1254)[277], *Rogiate* (1270)[575], *Rogyete* (1314)[576], *ecclesia de Roge(r)ate* (c1348)[238], *Roggeyate* (1419)[576], *Rogyet* (1567)[154], *Rogeat* (1577)[8], *Rogyate* (1628)[578].

This village lies 1 mile W of Caldicot, on the road to Newport. Charles[576] has suggested that the second element may be OE *gaet* 'gate' and the first OE *hyrygg* 'ridge' though the name has also been derived[579] from OE *ro* 'roe deer' (Ekwall[580] gives the meaning of *Rogate* Sussex as 'gate for roe deer'). But in Welsh OE *gaet* becomes *yet* or *yate*(*) appearing here as *iet* or *yet* or *yate.*

The first element appears to be *Rog,* a shortened form of the p.n. *Roger,* giving 'Roger's Gate.'

(*) Cornish *yet*[581]

ST 495916

Runston

Ecclesiam de Runestun qui apellatur sladforlung (1245-53)[582], *Ryngeston* (1262)[583], *Reneston* (c1291)[468], *Runston* (1374)[584] (1577)[8], *Runstone* (1585)[585].

This place lies SW of Chepstow. It was once a village with a church, but the village was depopulated in the early part of the 18th Century and the church became a ruin.

Charles[584] has suggested a derivation from OE *tun (-ton)* 'farm' or 'estate' and the OE p.n. *Runhere.* But the W p.n. *Rhun*[586] or *Run* seems more likely(*), so 'Rhun's Estate.'

(*) there is a reference to 'iouan, son of run....... of cairguent' (1071-5)[587].

ST 518984

St. Arvans

ecclesiam sanctorum iarmen et febric (955)[588], *sancto Aruino* (1193-1218)[128], *Sancto Arunno* (1223)[534], *(Walter de) Seint Eruan* (1306)[554], *ecclesia de sancto Aruyno* (c1348)[238], *St. Arvyn* (1361)[227], *Seynt Aruane* (1434)[591], *S. Aruan* (c1610)[27].

This village is some 2 miles N of Chepstow; this locality was once a grange (monastic farm) belonging to Tintern Abbey. The name has been taken from the church. But little seems to be known about St. Arvan (Arfan)[592].

ST 429896

St. Brides Netherwent (Saint-y-brid)

eccluis Santbreit, ecclesiam brigide (c895)[593], *ecclesia de sancta Brigida* (1193-1218)[128], *St. Brides* (1239)[594], *Sancta Brigida* (1254)[347], *Sce Brigide* (c1291)[6], *saint-y-brid* (c1566)[28], *Bryde* (1568)[595], *St. Bryde* (c1610)[27].

This is a village and parish between Magor and Penhow, the site of a medieval village. The church is dedicated to St. Bridget, an Irish saint who became very popular in Wales[596].

The suffix Netherwent or Lower Gwent (from Gwent Iscoed) is used to distinguish this church from the other St. Bride's in Gwent, i.e. St. Bride's Wentloog.

The name also occurs in Welsh form as *Llansanffraed* (nr. Abergavenny, from W *llan* 'church' W *san(t)* 'saint' and W *Braid* = *Ffraid* = Bridget).

ST 325895

St. Julians (Sain Silian)

Demerthir ivn et AARON ..territorium, sanctorum martirum iulij et aaron (c864)[606], *ecclesiam Sancti Julii et Aaron atque Alban* (1201)[607], *Julii et Aron* (1290)[607], *Saynt Julyane* (1576)[608], *Sainte Julians Sainct Julyans* (1583)[609], *S. Ielian* (c1610)[27], *St. Julians* (1622)[610].

Now a suburb of Newport, on the road to Caerleon, this was originally the name of a manor house, home of the Herbert family. But the house took its name from an early chapel dedicated to one of the two saints reputedly the first to be martyred at Caerleon in Roman times (AD304)[611].

St. Kynmark (Llangynfarch)

Lann Cinmarch, ecclesiam Cynmarchi (c625)[597], *lanncinuarch* (c722)[598], *uillam lann cinmarch* (1128)[35], *St. Kynemarch* (1193-1218 or 1254)[163], *Seint Wynemark* (c1291)[6], *St. Kynmark, St. Kinmark* (1584/5)[599].

Possibly the only existing reminder of this place is the Chepstow road name Kingmarch Road. But this was the name of the earliest church in Chepstow, established some 400-500 years before the Norman Conquest. Afterwards it became an Augustinian foundation. It was last used in 1642 and has now disappeared. It appears to have been situated to the N of Chepstow near 'The Mount.'

The church took its name from *Cynfarch Oer,* a 5th Century British prince and disciple of St. Dyfrig[600].

SO 461171

St. Maughans

lannmocha Lann Bocha (c860)[601], *lann Bocha lannmocha* (c860)[602], *lannmocha* (c1025)[603](1072)[604], *ecclesia de sancto Machuto* (c1348)[5], *Sct. Moughan* (1577)[8].

The village (St. Maughan's Green) lies approximately 3 miles N of Rockfield nr. Monmouth. The name has come from the church which is dedicated to St. Malo or Machuto[605].

St. Pierre (Sain Pyr)

ST 514905

sancto Petro (apud Portecuith) (1193-1218)[128], *sancto petro* (1245-53)[582], *ecclesia de sancto Petro* (c1348)[543], *Seint Pere by Marthern* (1374)[613], *Seynt Pere* (1490)[614].

This is a mansion house near Mathern with a gatehouse dating back to the 14th or 15th Century, all that remains of an older building.

Bradney derives the name from the Norman family of St. Pierre who settled here. But references [128] and [582] above refer to a church of St. Peter which seems to be in this locality, and this church may, in fact, be the origin of the name which later appears in French (St. Pierre), and as a family name.

Shirenewton (Drenewydd Gelli-Farch)

ST 478937

Newton (1148-83)[615], *Nova Villa* (1254)[277], *Sherrevesneuton* (1287)[572], *Sherevesneuton* (1323)[617], *Ecc'ia de Schirreues newton* (c1348)[618], *Shere Newton* (1497)[619], *Shirenewton* (1610)[27].

The village of Shirenewton lies some 3 miles from Chepstow, on the road to Usk. It was once a manor granted to the Sheriff of Gloucester in 1090 AD, hence the name from OE *Sci gerefa* 'sheriff' (i.e. the representative of royal authority in a shire) and OE *tun (-ton)* 'estate', used here in the sense of 'manor', i.e. 'the sheriff's new manor' (i.e. 'new' in 1090!).

The Welsh name is from W *tre(f)* = *dre* 'estate' or 'farm', W *newydd* 'new' and W *gelli* 'grove.' The last element W *march* = *farch* 'stallion' gives 'the new estate of the stallion's grove.' This seems rather odd.

But W *march* 'stallion' may, in fact, refer to the Celtic goddess Epona (later W *Rhiannon*) who was reputed to appear in the form of a horse or stallion. The grove may have been the place where this goddess was worshipped or venerated

SO 457203

Skenfrith (Ynysgynwraidd)

Ynys Gynwreid (1215)[620], *Skenfrede* (1250)[621], *Skynefrith* (c1291)[6], *Skenwrethe* (1535)[38], *Skenfreth, Skenefrethe* (1543-4)[622], *Skenffrith* (c1610)[27].

The village of Skenfrith which has an imposing Norman castle, is on the River Monnow, on the NE border of Gwent. The name is from W *ynys* 'island' but also, as in this case, 'water-meadow' (flat land beside a river) and the W p.n. *Cynwraidd*[623] = *Gwnwraidd,* so 'Cynwraidd's water-meadow'. The Welsh name *Ynysgynwraidd* has become 'Skenfrith'!

SO 311213

Stanton

Stanton (1293)[624], *Stanton chap.* (1577)[8].

This hamlet near Llanvihangel Crucorney (N of Abergavenny) was once a Manor belonging to Llanthony Priory. The name is clearly from OE *ston* 'stone' and OE *tun (-ton)* 'estate' or 'farm' or 'enclosure' and the meaning has been given as 'stone town'[625]. But the name Staunton is also found near Coleford in Gloucestershire. This place is near a prominent stone (The Buckstone) so the most likely meaning is 'farm or enclosure near the stone.' But in 'Place-Names of Gloucestershire'[626], 'stony farm-stead' is given. Ekwall[627] says that the name is '*tun* on stony ground' or that it has come 'from some prominent stone or stones nearby.' It is not clear whether this name has come from this other Staunton or from some prominent stone nearby (*Cwm coed-y-cerrig,* from W *cerrig,* plural of *carreg* 'rock', is nearby).

ST 505875

Sudbrook

Suthe broch (1193-1218)[128], *Sutbroc* (1333)[629], *ecclesia de Sudebrok* (c1348)[543], *Sudbroke* (1548/9)[630], *Sudbrok* (c1610)[27], *Southbrook* (c1836)[212].

The village of Sudbrook lies near the Gwent end of the Severn Rail Tunnel. An Iron-Age hill-fort on a promontory guards an ancient cross-channel landing place. This was once a medieval village with a Norman church (now ruined). Houses were built here at the end of the 19th Century for workers on the Severn Tunnel.

The name was originally that of a small brook nearby, i.e. South brook or Sudbrook (in some forms, from OE *sud* 'south').

There is a Southbrook in Herefordshire and this name has arisen in the same way.

SO 533000

Tintern (Tyndyrn)

Dindyrn, ryt tindyrn, tindirn (c620)[631], *ecclesia de tynderna* (late c14)[632], *Tinterna* (1131)[633], *Tyntern* (1267)[634], *Tinternam* (1314)[136], *(Abbas de) Tynterna* (c1348)[512], *Tyntern* (c1610)[27].

This village on the River Wye is renowned for its magnificent ruined Cistercian Abbey (parts date back to 1131 AD).

The name is from W *din* 'fortress' and W *teyrn* 'King' i.e. 'the royal fortress.' The actual site of this place is unknown but it may have been situated on one of the high points near Tintern. The name is associated with Tewdrig, a King of Gwent in the 5th Century.

SO 531008

Tintern Parva

agrum Louhai, drec din dirn (c765)[635], *ecclesia de Parua Tynterna* (c1348)[238].

This is Tintern Village; houses to the N of the Abbey. It is difficult to realise that, last century, this was an industrial area with a wireworks. Nearby, in the Anghidy Valley, there are the remains of small blast furnaces of early date.

The name is from Tintern (see previous paqe) and L *parva* 'little' or 'small' i.e. 'Little Tintern.'

SO 418102

Tregare (Tre'r-gaer)

Tregear (1285)[650], *Tregayr* (c1353)[651], *Treirgair, Treyrgayr* (1490)[653], *Tregare* (1523)[477], *trer gaer* (c1566)[28], *Treeargaire* (1600)[654], *Treargaire* (c1610)[27].

This village, with houses widely dispersed, lies to the N of Raglan. The church stands on a slight eminence which may have been the site of a hill-fort, hence the name from W *tre(f)* 'farm' 'estate' or 'enclosure' and W *caer* = gaer 'hill-fort' i.e. 'the enclosure or estate (near the) hill-fort'.

Tregaer Church viewed from the N.W.

Trelleck; the three prehistoric standing stones.

SO 500055

Trelleck (Tryleg)

trylec bechan (c698)[636], *ecclesiam Trilecc* (c755)[637], *Ecclesia Trylec* (c755)[638], *podo mainuon in medlo trilec (c960)*[639], *Trillec* (1230-40)[458], *Trillek* (1254)[277], *Trilleck maner* (1295)[14], *Trillet* (1314)[136], *Trilleck* (1524)[640], *Trelech* (1548)[641](1763)[170], *Trylegh* (1577)[8].

Trelleck village lies to the S of Monmouth on the road to Devauden and Chepstow. It was once much larger than at present (note the size of the church) but was de-populated in the 14th Century. It is famous for the three menhirs (standing stones) known as Harold's Stones. Bradney[642] derives the name, quite incorrectly, from W *tre(f)* and W *llech* 'flat stone' to give 'stone town'. But from the name-forms, the first element is very clearly OW *try* W *tri* 'three'. Combination with W *llech* would give 'the three stone(s)', a probable reference to the three menhirs aforementioned.

As has been pointed out[643], W *llech* being a feminine noun requires a change of W *tri* to *tair.* But this may not be really valid since in early Welsh, the genders of nouns were not always the same as at present and rules of mutation were not the same. For instance, W *nant* 'stream' (originally 'valley') is also a feminine noun but the form *trineint* is found in the early literature[644]. So 'the three stones.'

SO 492017

Trelleck Grange (Tryleg Grange)

Ecclesia mainuon id est uilla guicon (c96())[645], *uillam guidcon* (c960)[646], *Ecclesia Trylec Lann Mainuon* (c755)[638], *Cil Wyddon*[648], *Trilegh Grange* (c1610)[27], *Treleck Grange* (1787)[131].

Now a hamlet with a church, approximately 2 miles S of Trelleck, this was once a grange (monastic farm) of Tintern Abbey, hence the name.

The earliest name-form is from L *villa* 'estate' and the p.n. *Guicon* or *Guidcon* (probably *Gwyddon*). The p.n. Gwyddon is found elsewhere e.g. Nant Gwyddon, Abercarn.

SO 375045

Trostrey (Trostre)

Trestray (1295)[14], *Trostraxhen* (1314)[136], *Trostre* (c1348)[106], *trosdre* (c1566)[28], *Trostrey* (1570)[17].

The village of Trostrey is some 2 miles to the N of Usk town; the houses are dispersed over a wide area. A moated manor site being excavated may have been the centre for a somewhat scattered *tre(f)*.

The name is from W *traws* 'across', 'over', 'above' or 'beyond' and W *tre(f)* 'homestead with land' then 'group of homesteads', so '(the place) above or beyond the *tre(f)*.'

The name is found elsewhere, e.g. Trostre Steelworks, Llanelli.

SO 509113

Troy

lordship of Troi (1148-83)[655], *Troia* (1193-1218)[128](1245-53)[224], *Troie* (1254)[277], *Ecclia de Troy* (c1291)[6], *Troy maner Troy ecclia* (1295)[14], *Troye* (1314)[136], *Ecc'ia de Troia cum Capellano* (c1348)[512], *Troy* (1577)[8].

Now the name of a mansion house and nearby hamlet 1 mile S of Monmouth, near the confluence of the Troy (Troddi) brook with the Wye. The name has come from the brook, Troy being a form of W *Tro(dd)i.* Mitchell Troy (which see), the village about a mile upstream is on land once part of the Lordship of Troi (Troy).

ST 540945

Tutshill

This village lies across the Wye from Chepstow; it is actually in Gloucestershire. The name is from OE *twt* 'look-out' and OE *hyll* 'hill', i.e. 'the look-out hill' (a border observation post?).

The name is found elsewhere, e.g. Twt Hill, Flintshire[656].

ST 440870

Undy (Gwyndy)

uillam iunuhic (c1015)[667], *Wondy* (1245-53)[224](1314)[136], *Woundy* (1291)[6], *ecclesia de Wondy* (c1348)[238], *Wondy otherwise Undy* (1559)[668], *gwndi* (c1566)[28], *Woudye* (1577)[8], *Undy* (1787)[131].

The village of Undy is on the Caldicot Levels, E of Magor. It was once the possession of Sir Howell ap Iorwerth, Lord of Caerleon; he was dispossessed by Sir William de St. Maur in 1240 AD.

The earliest name is from L *villa* 'estate' and the p.n. *Iunuhic;* this may very possibly be a form of the W p.n. *(G)wyndy*[669] (or *Gwyndaf),* reputedly the founder of the church here.

That forms such as *Wondy* and *Undy* have come from *(G)wyndy* seems probable. However, the word *gwyndy* appears in a different context in the early literature. In the Privilegium of St. Teilo[670], there is a reference to *Gundy Teiliau.* At first sight this word *gundy (gwyndy)* appears to be an inverted form of W *tŷ gwyn* 'white house.' But it seems to have meant 'meeting place' or 'court'[671] or 'stone chapel'[672]. Either meaning of *gwyndy* could be relevant here.

SO 375005

Usk (Brynbuga)

Bullaeum (C2)[657], *Burrio* (C3)[657], *Din Birrion* (c765)[658], *Lisdin Borrion* (c1100)[659], *Huscha* (1086)[685], *(river) Usch* (1146)[660], *Oscham* (1214)[661], *Usc* (1193-1214, 1254)[163], *Uske maner* (1295)[14], *Uske* (1314)[136], *Vske* (1577)[8], *Brinbiga* (1405)[662], *Brynn buga* (c1566)[663], *Uske so called Burrium of Antoninus called by the Welsh Brynbuga* (1684)[686].

This historic town in the Usk Valley has a ruined castle on a prominent site. The medieval town was planned and built by Richard de Clare between 1154-70 the lay-out owing nothing to the previous Roman occupation[664] (there was a Roman fort here in the 1st Century). The Charter dates to 1398 and the place was a Corporate Borough before this. Usk was the site of a Benedictine Nunnery.

The form *Bullaeum* mentioned by Ptolemy is apparently dubious (l and r may have been confused) and the earliest reliable nameform appears to be the *Burrio* of the 3rd Century Antonine Itinerary; this is said to have come from the Gaulish p.n. *Burros*[657].

The Norman town took its name from the river; the origin of the river name is still somewhat controversial[665 666].

The Welsh name *Bryn Buga* is from W *bryn* 'hill' and clearly refers to the hill on which Usk castle stands. However, the meaning of *buga* is less clear.

A derivation from W *big* 'pointed' has been suggested. Bradney (HM. iii p.114) quotes a work which mentions 'Buga gawr'; this implies that Buga was a personal name (of a giant!).Ellis[714] notes that the earliest reference to the *Biga (Afon Biga)* in

Brynbuga (Usk), The giant Buga views his domain!
Fe! Fo! Fi! and Fum! I am the giant Buga. Take care how you pronounce my name! For it should rhyme with meagre.

Montgomeryshire (Trefaldwyn) is in the form *Cwm Buga* (1420) and he also concludes that *Buga* was a personal name. Another possibility which has been advanced is that the word may have come from W *bugeilio* "to watch" (from which the word W *bugail* "shepherd" is derived); hence "look-out hill".

ST 381833

Whitson

Wytteston (c1291)[6], *Wadestone* (1314)[136], *Wyduston* (1358)[674], *Wytston* (1577)[8], *Witston* (1582)[673], *Whitson* (1836)[212].

The hamlet of Whitson lies near Goldcliff (nr. Newport). The name has been derived from the OE p.n. *Hwita* and OE *tun* (-ton) 'farm' or 'estate', i.e. 'Hwita's farm or estate.'

ST 411878

Wilcrick

Willecric (1231-4)[705], *Wildecrik* (1254)[347], *Wilkricke* (1270)[707], *Wilcrick* (1271)[706], *Wildcrik* (1314)[136], *ecclesia de Wylde cryk* (c1348)[543], *Wilcricke* (1589)[676], *Willcrick* (1787)[131], *Y Feolcrug* (c1733)[677].

This hamlet is near Magor, near a hill-fort on a prominence rising to over 200 feet; this may have been a major hill-fort of the Silures. The name is from the hill-fort, from British *cruc* (W *crug*, OE *cryk*) 'mound'. The earliest name-forms appear to have no *d;* this suggests a derivation from W *gwylio* 'to watch' giving 'the look out mound'. The forms with *d* suggest a derivation from W *(g)wyllt* 'wild', 'overgrown' 'abandoned' (OE *wilde* means the same thing) but the real origin of this may be W *gwyl* above. The later Welsh form *Y Feolgrug* is from W *moel* = *foel* 'bare' ie. 'the bare mound'.

Wilcrick viewed from the N.

ST 454997

Wolvesnewton (Llanwynell)

Nova Villa (1254)[495], *Wlnesneuton* (1295)[14], *ecclesia de Noua villa lupi* (c1348)[106], *Wolvisnewton* (1408)[689], *Wolfeneuton* (1577)[8], *Wolvenewton* (c1790)[135].

Wolvesnewton lies on a minor road between Llangwm and Devauden, at the foot of a hill with a hill-fort atop, hence the W name *Trenewydd dan-y-gaer* 'the new estate below the hill-fort.'

The earliest name-form is from L *nova* 'new' and L *villa* 'estate' with the addition (c1348) of L *lupi* 'wolves' but here referring to a family named Wolf, so 'The Wolfs' new estate.'

The English form is from the family name Wolf, OE *niew* 'new and OE *tun (-ton)* 'estate'; it means the same thing.

The *lan gunhoill* (c970) mentioned in the Book of Llandaff[678] was in the Wolvesnewton area; name-forms are: *Languonhoill* (1119)[679], well of *St. Gwynhael* (1425)[680], parish of *Lanvanell otherwise Wolvesnewton* (1553)[681]. The W name *Llanwynell* reflects this.

SO 486108

Wonastow (Llanwarw)

Gyrthebiriuc Lanngunguarui super Trodi, ecclesiam gurthebiriuc (c750)[682], *Ec. Gurthebiriuc id est L Gunguarui, or Wonwarrowstow* (c14)[683], *Sancti Wengel* (1254)[51], *Wolwarestowe* (c1291)[6], *ecclesia de Wonewarestowe* (c1348)[5], *Wonewastowe* (1415)[684], *Wonastow* (1483)[294](1577)[8], *Wonastowe* (1493)[687].

This village lies approximately 2 miles SW of Monmouth. The original name is from L *ecclesia* 'church' and the p.n. *Gurthebiriuc* (Vortimer). This has then become *Lanngungari* from W *llan* 'church' and the p.n. *Gungari* or *Guingualoeus* a form of the name of St. Winwaloe[688] (Gwyngary). *Wonwarrowstowe* is an Anglicised form in which Winwaloe is followed by OE *stowe* 'meeting place' but used here in the same sense as W *llan*. Thus, both English and Welsh forms mean 'Church of St. Winwaloe.' *Wonastow* is an abbreviated form of *Wonwarrowstowe.* The saint's name Winwaloe is very variable, appearing in more than 50 forms including Venole, Gweune, Gwenny and Gwarrog[688].

Winwaloe, reputedly a son of Brychan, King of Bycheiniog was born in Brittany and is commemorated there (Monastery of Landevennie). In Gwent, besides Wonastow, the now extinct chapels of Llandevenny and Llanwinney were dedicated to this saint.

References

Abbreviations

AC	Annales Cambriae, J. Williams ab Ithel, 1860.
APDBIW	The Account of the Progress of His Grace, Henry the Duke of Beaufort Through Wales in 1684, Thomas Dineley, 1888.
Arch. Camb.	Archeologia Cambrensis (1846-)
BBCS	Bulletin of the Board of Celtic Studies (1921-)
BDD	Badminton Deeds and Documents (1-270, 1946)
BL	The Book of Llan Dâv, ed., J. Gwenogvryn Evans, (1893).
BMR	Badminton Manorial Records (Vols. 2 and 3, 1946)
BPNHS	British Place-Names in Their Historical Setting, E. McClure, (1910).
BT	Brut y Tywysogyon, Red Book of Hergest Version, ed. T. Jones, (1955).
CAM	Cartae et alia Munimenta quae ad dominium de Glamorganicia pertinet, ed. G.T. Clark (2nd ed., 1910).
CAPRW	Calendar of Ancient Petitions Relating to Wales. W. Rees, (1975).
CARWM	Records of the Court of Augmentations Relating to Wales and Monmouthshire, ed. E.A. Lewis and J. Conway Davies, (1954).
CChR	Calendar of Charter Rolls
CEEP	The Chief Elements used in English Place-Names. A. Mawer, (1924).
CIPM	Calendarium Inquisitorium Post Mortem. Vol.I, (1806).

CKD	Calendar of the Kemeys Documents, 3 Vols, (1949).
CPE	A Popular Dictionary of Cornish Place-Names, O.J. Padel, (1988).
CPNE	Dictionary of Cornish Place-Name Elements, O.J. Padel, (1985).
CPR	Calendar of Patent Rolls
DB	Domesday Book, Henry Ellis (British Museum), 1916.
DL	The Diocese of Llandaff in 1763, J.R. Guy, (1991).
DP	The Description of Pembrokeshire by George Owen, ed. Henry Owen, (1892-1936).
EANC	Enwau Afonydd a Nentydd Cymru, R.J. Thomas (1938).
EARWD	Episcopal Acts Relating to Welsh Dioceses, 1066-72, J. Conway Davies, (2 Vols, 1948).
ECPCW	An Inventory of Early Chancery Proceedings Concerning Wales, E.A. Lewis, (1937).
EEA	English Episcopal Acts (Canterbury), (1991).
EFN	English Field Names: A Dictionary, J. Field, (1989).
EPCW	Exchequer Proceedings Concerning Wales, Emyr and Gwynne Jones, (1939).
ETD	The Place-Names of Gwent, Canon E.T. Davies (1982).
EWM	'An Early Welsh Microcosm'; Studies in the Llandaff Charters, Wendy Davies, 1978.
FPN	Flintshire Place-Names, Rev. Ellis Davies, (1959).
GAHW	A Guide to Ancient and Historic Wales: Glamorgan and Gwent. Elisabeth Whittle, (1992).
Gir	Giraldi Cambrensis, Opera 6, Itinerarium Kambriae et Descriptio Kambriae, (Rolls Series, London, 1868).
GPC	Geriadur Prifysgol Cymru.
HM	A History of Monmouthshire from the Coming of the Normans to the Present Time, Sir J.A. Bradney, (4 Vols, 1904-33).
HPLB	History of the Parish of Llanwern and Bishton. Rev. S. Jones, (1967)
IPM (1925)	Inquisitio Post Mortem of Gilbert de Clare (2nd) (also in 'Edward 2nd in Glamorgan', Rev. J. Griffith, 1904, Appendix D, p.22).
IPM (1314)	Inquisitio Post Mortem of Gilbert de Clare (3rd) CIPM I pp.265-66 (also in 'Edward 2nd in Glamorgan', Rev. J. Griffith, 1904, Appendix E, p.23).

IW	Itinerary through Wales by John Leland (Extracted MS) ed. Toulmin-Smith, (1906).
JCH	John Capel Hanbury: Collection of Deeds of the Hanbury Estate (GCRO).
JFLT	Jones family of Llanover and Treowen (D2-D583, 1967).
JHSCW	Journal of the Historical Society of the Church in Wales.
KT	Kemeys - Tynte Papers.
LEA	Llandaff Episcopal Acta 1140-1287, ed. D. Crouch, (1985).
LBS	The Lives of the British Saints, S. Baring Gould and J. S. Fisher, (4 Vols., from 1907).
LCBS	The Lives of the Cambro-British Saints, Rev. W.J. Rees, (1853).
LCTC	The Lordship, Castle and Town of Chepstow, J.G. Wood, (1910).
Lib. Land	Liber Landavensis, W.J. Rees, (1840).
MA	The Myvyrian Archiaology of Wales, 2nd Ed., (1870).
MB	The Maindee Book, H. Clark, (1985).
MD	Milbourne Documents.
MHT	Monmouthshire; History and Topography, C.J.O. Evans, (1953).
MLSW	The Marcher Lordship of South Wales, 1415-1536, Selected Documents, T.B. Pugh, (1963).
MM	The Mapping of Monmouthshire, D.P.M. Michael, (1985).
Med. Mon	Medieval Monmouth, K.E. Kissack, (1974).
Mon	Monastican Anglicanum, Sir William Dugdale, (1846).
MR	Monmouthshire Reviews (1933, 1934).
NCPNW	The Non-Celtic Place-Names in Wales. B.G. Charles, (1938).
NM	Newport Collection of MS, GCRO.
NT	Valuation of Norwich, ed. W. E. Lunt, (1926).
NTCB	The Names of Towns and Cities in Britain, M. Gelling, W.H.F. Nicolaisen and M. Richards, (1970).
NU	Norman Usk; The Birth of a Town, A.G. Mein, 1986.
ODPN	The Concise Oxford Dictionary of English Place-Names, Eilert Ekwall, (1960).
PM	Peniarth Manuscript.
PNDP	The Place-Names of Dinas Powys Hundred, Prof. G.O. Pierce, (1968).
PNG	The Place-Names of Gloucestershire, A.H. Smith, (4 Vols, 1964).

PNH	Herefordshire Place-Names, B. Copelstone - Crow, (1989).
PNLL	Place-Names in the Living Landscape, M. Gelling, (1984).
PNP	The Place-Names of Pembrokeshire, B.G. Charles, (2 Vols, 1993).
PNRB	The Place-Names of Roman Britain, A.L.F. Rivett and Colin Smith, (1979).
PNT	Taxatio Ecclesiastica Anglicae et Walliae Auctoritate, P. Nicholas IV c.1291 (1801 ed).
PNWG	The Place-Names of Western Gwent, G.O. Osborne and G.J. Hobbs, (1992).
SBMR	Schedule of Badminton Manuscript and Records (Group 2), M. Griffiths, (1965).
SCP	Catalogue of Star Chamber Proceedings Relating to Wales, Ifan ap owen Edwards, (1929).
SDLLW	Survey of Duchy Lancaster Lordships in Wales, 1609-1613, William Rees, (1953).
St. P and M	Catalogue of Documents relating to the St. Pierre Estate, Malpas; Miss Protheroe Deeds, (1966).
SWM	South Wales and the March, 1284-1415, W. Rees. (1924).
SWMRS	South Wales and Monmouthshire Record Society.
TPM	Tredegar Park Muniments.
VE	Valor Ecclesiasticus Tempus Henr. 8. (1535) (Record Commission, London, 1802).
VSBG	Vitae Santorum Britanniae et Genealogie, A.W. Wade-Evans, (1994).
W	Appendix (by T. Wakeman) to LCBS.
WCD	A Welsh Classical Dictionary; People in History and Legend up to about 1000AD, P.C. Bartrum, 1993.

1 PNRB, p.39
2 BT, p.158
3 Gir, 6, p.47
4 EARWD, 2, p.691
5 BL, p.320
6 PNT p278
7 NM, 412.6, (5156)
8 MM, p.65
9 PM 147, p.919
10 NTCB, p.37
11 BBCS, 35, (1988), p.53
12 EFN, p.12
13 LEA, p.56
14 IPM (de Clare, 1295)
15 HM, 4, p.159
16 KT 1, p.2
17 NM, 424.5 (4282)
18 CPNE, p.289
19 PNP, p.531
20 CPNE, p.183
21 JFLT, p.165 (5140)
22 SBMR, p.217
23 BMR, 2, p.14
24 BMR, 2, p.18
25 NM, 413, (5136)
26 NM, 416, (5233)
27 MM, p.68
28 PM 147, p.920
29 HM, 2, p.112
30 HM, 3, p.3
31 PNG, 3, p.243
32 HM, 2, p.212
33 BL p.180, EWM p.174
34 BL, p.90
35 BL, p.31,32
36 BL, pp.43,44
37 CAPRW, p.21
38 VE, 4, pp. 345-78
39 EFN, p.25
40 NM, 431 (2544)
41 MM, p.102
42 MM, p.103
43 LBS, 2, p.43
44 NCPNW, p.114
45 ODPN, p.46
46 BL, pp.141, 340
47 PNG, 3, p.233
48 ODPN, p.68
49 PNLL, p.15
50 EANC, p.42
51 NT, p.317
52 CAPRW, p.267
53 NM, 412.6 (5207)
54 JCH, 2, p.185 (1410)
55 HM, 2, p.103
56 FPN, p.18
57 PNH, p.165
58 PNP, p.165
59 Arch. Camb., 1855, pp. 14-17
60 GAHW, p.47
61 PNDP, pp.71, 201
62 GAHW, p.36
63 GAHW, p.41
64 GAHW, p.64
65 TPM, 58-76, p.1306
66 DP, 1, p.216; 2, p.387
67 FPN, p.26
68 PNRB, p.493
69 'Historia Brittonum', Nennius, Rev. W. Gunn, (1819)
70 BL, p.220
71 EARWD, 2, p.608
72 HM, 4, p.3
73 LEA, p.5
74 LEA, p.68
75 DB, p.162
76 EARWD, 2, p.661
77 LEA, p.57

78 LEA, p.58
79 NM, 421.3 (6141)
80 NM, 421.3 (7089)
81 CEEP, p.18
82 NCPNW, p.242
83 FPN, pp. 29-30
84 HM, 4, p.160
85 BL, p.236, EWM, p.183
86 BL, p.198, EWM, p.177
87 MON, 7, p.1022
88 NCPNW, p.247
89 SWM, p.12
90 CAPRW, pp.148,149
91 HM, 4, p.205
92 St. P & M, p.96 (D5O1. 443)
93 W, p.13
94 BL, p.158, EWM, p.170
95 ODPN, p.100
96 NTCB, p.71
97 MHT, p.258
98 GAHW, pp.47, 48
99 BPNHS, p.34
100 NCPNW, p.243
101 BL, pp.209, 376
102 NCPNW, p.244
103 SWMRS, 2, p.102
104 SBMR, p.218
105 JFLT, p.71 (5318)
106 BL, p.321
107 NM, 413 (2029)
108 NM, 413 (5136)
109 NM, 413 (4974)
110 DL, p.165
111 HM, 2, p.114
112 W, p.8
113 NT p.318
114 HM, 4, p.272
115 HM, 4, p.296
116 SCP, p.113
117 TPM, 77-86, p.1495
118 NM, 432 (5799)
119 HM, 4, p.304
120 GPC, p.542
121 NCPNW, p.39
122 PNP, p.421
123 BL, p.262, EWM, p.187
124 NM, 431.3, (4556)
125 JCH, 1, p.37 (0402)
126 EARWD, 2, p.669
127 CIPM, 1, p.251
128 LEA, p.39
129 LEA, p.83
130 NM, 421.3 (5559)
131 MM, p.85
132 LBS, 4, pp.25, 26
133 'A Middle Bronze Age Barrow at Crick, Mon', H. M. Savory, Arch. Camb.,1940 p.169,170
134 BL, p.224
135 BDD, 1, p.24
136 IPM (1314)
137 EANC, p.50
138 EANC, p.49
139 ODPN, p.287
140 'A Dictionary of the Welsh Language' William Owen (Pughe), 1803
141 EARWD, 1, p.251
142 EARWD, 1, p.261
143 ECPCW, p.234
144 EPCW, pp.260
145 EPCW, p.261
146 HM, 1, p.233
147 EANC, p.120
148 SWMRS, 2, p.118
149 Geriadur Llogell, W. Richards, 1861
150 HM, 3, p.171
151 BL, p.282
152 BDD, 1, p.81

153 BDD, 1, p.121
154 HM, 4, pp.11,163
155 HM, 3, p.116
156 LEA, p.20
157 LEA, p.35
158 EARWD, 2, p.734
159 CAPRW p.21
160 NM, 421.3 (7089)
161 NM, 423.4 (5622)
162 BL, p.227, EWM p.182
163 EARWD, 2, p.696
164 NCPNW, p.267
165 JFLT, p.16 (D583.12)
166 JFLT, p.53 (D2.31)
167 NM, 442 (5094)
168 LBS, 2, p.343
169 HM, 4, p.181
170 NM, 423.4, (5626)
171 HM, 4, p.176
172 CAPRW, p.102 (3360)
173 HM, 4, p.246
174 HM, 4, p.10
175 BL, pp.32, 44, 182
176 LBS, 3, p.377
177 BL, p.183, EWM, p.174
178 BL, p.231
179 BL, p.275, 276
180 LCTC, pp.47, 48
181 JFLT, p.126 (5089)
182 LBS, 4, p.288
183 HM, 4, p.159
184 Arch. Camb., 1910, p.310
185 St. P and M, p.93, D501.413
186 BMR, 3, p.257 (2350)
187 Arch. Camb., 1910, pp.305, 309
188 HM, 4, p.114
189 EARWD, 2, p.618
190 EARWD, 2, p.672
191 EARWD, 2, p.673
192 Gir, 6, p.56
193 CAM, 3, p.859
194 EARWD, 2, p.733
195 LEA, p.64
196 MLSW, p.44
197 ECPCW, p.220
198 NCPNW, p.245
199 Trans. Geol. Soc., Ser.2, Vol.I, (1824), p.305
200 Mem. Geol. Soc., Vol.3, p.122
201 Quarterly Journal, 61, (1905), p.374.
202 PNLL, p.374
203 NCPNW, p.260
204 EARWD, 2, p.713
205 BL, p.327
206 MM, p.87
207 NM, 423.4 (5630)
208 SWMRS, 3, p.30
209 NM, 415 (5184)
210 NM, 415 (5230)
211 ECPCW, p.240
212 MM, p.111
213 NCPNW, p.259
214 ODPN, p.207
215 BDD, I, p.26
216 SCP, p.99
217 ECPCW, p.271
218 NM, 390 (3577)
219 EARWD, 1, p.247
220 CKD, 2, p.158, (5868)
221 NM, 417.6 (2420)
222 Lib. Land, p.330
223 Arch. Camb., 1875, pp.70-73
224 BL, p.318
225 CEEP, p.64
226 BL, p.261, EWM, p.187
227 HM, 4, p.8
228 HM, 4, p.8
229 St. P and M. p.99, (D501.145)

230 BL, p.143, EWM, p.168
231 Mon, 5, p.268
232 BL, p.323
233 HM, 4, p.23
234 LBS, 3, p.157
235 BL, p.403
236 EARWD, 2, p.632
237 ODPN, p.254
238 BL, p.322
239 BMR, 2, p.218
240 HM, 4, p.98
241 NCPNW, pp.246, 247
242 BL, p.122
243 LBS, 3, p.290
244 BL, p.172, EWM, p.172
245 HM, 4, p.147
246 HM, 4, p.165
247 TPM, 87-89, p.1776
248 NCPNW, p.246
249 LBS, 1, p.116
250 BL, p.321 (Index p.391)
251 'An Historical Tour of Monmouthshire' Rev. W. Coxe (1904 ed), p.161
252 BL, p.183, EWM, p.177
253 BL, pp.198, 200
254 BDD, 1, p.28
255 GPC, p.397
256 HM, 4, p.109
257 PNP, p.25
258 BL, p.179, EWM, p.173
259 BDD, 1, p.22
260 EARWD, 1, p.272
261 BL, p.166, EWM, p.272
262 BL, p.175, EWM, p.135
263 PNG, 3, p.263
264 DP, 3, p.189
265 HM, 4, p.273
266 PNT p.160
267 HM, 4, p.287
268 NM, 160, D43 (3488)
269 TPM, 1-45, p.420
270 'The Place-Name Liswerry', J. Herbert, Introducing Monmouthshire, 38, p.8
271 LBS, 2, p.52
272 PNWG, p.35
273 EEA, 3, p.136
274 LEA, p.64
275 DP, 4, p.424
276 MLSW, p.51
277 NT, p.321
278 BMR, 2, p.224
279 HM, 4, p.13
280 'Tintern's Story', Judith Russell
281 GPC, p.2244
282 Bibliography of Monmouth Borough (Compiled in Newport Borough Library, pp.3550)
283 BL, p.121
284 BL, p.180
285 BL, p.225
286 NM, 416 (5159)
287 Gir, 6, p.37
288 BL, p.261, EWM, p.187
289 SCP, p.102
290 MM, p.71
291 BDD, 1, p.238
292 JFLT, p.108, (4916)
293 JFLT, p.150, (5237)
294 BDD, 1, p.99
295 HM, 1, p.283
296 NM, 416.8 (4899)
297 HM, 1, p.282
298 BL, p.207, EWM, p.179
299 BL, p.208, EWM, p.179
300 NM, 413 (2032)
301 LBS, 4, p.249
302 EARWD, 2, p.621

303 BDD, 1, p.70
304 SCP, p.102
305 LBS, 4, pp.214, 215
306 BL, p.255, EWM, p.186
307 HM, 4, p.214
308 NM, 426.5 (4435)
309 LBS, 4, pp.353-62
310 BL, p.166
311 BL, p.156, EWM, p.170
312 LBS, 4, p.35
313 BL, p.159, EWM, p.170
314 HM, 2, p.47
315 CIPM, p.65
316 LBS, 2, p.414
317 BL, p.192, EWM, p.176
318 PNH, p.134
319 LBS, 2, pp. 414, 415
320 BL, p.241, EWM, p.184
321 SWMRS, 4, p.10
322 NM, 443.5, (480)
323 NM, 443.5, (488)
324 BL, p.228
325 LBS, 3, p.433
326 SWMRS, 2, p.78
327 W. p.11
328 JCH, 1, p.26, (0627)
329 JCH, 1, p.27, (0632)
330 MM, p.79
331 EARWD, 2, p.718
332 MD, 1, p.50
333 'The Daughters of Brychan', T. Thomley Jones, Brycheiniog, 1976/7, 27, p.42
334 NM, 453.3 (5839)
335 NM, 453.3 (5840)
336 HM, 3, p.82
337 EWM, p.123
338 HPLB, p.12
339 BL, p.374
340 LBS, 2, p.247
341 BL, p.206, EWM, p.178
342 BL, p.284
343 HM, 2, p.8
344 JFLT, p.272 (4893)
345 LBS, 2, p.202
346 EARWD, 2, p.662
347 NT, p.320
348 NU, p.119
349 JHSCW, 27, p.9
350 BDD, 2, p.516 (148)
351 LBS, 2, pp.139-146
352 BL, p.252, EWM, p.185
353 BDD, 1, p .106 (1397)
354 NM, 423.6 (1102)
355 BL, p.410
356 LBS, 2, p.264
357 BL, p.173, EWM, p.172
358 BL, p.274
359 NM, 423.1 (4859)
360 MM, p.91
361 NM, 423.1 (1070)
362 NM, 423.1 (1073)
363 NM, 423.1 (1072)
364 BL, p.241, EWM, p.184
365 HM, 2, p.257
366 BDD, 1, p.51
367 HM, 2, p.54
368 LBS, 3, p.320
369 LEA, p.26
370 LBS, 3, p.387
371 BL, p.241, EWM, p.184
372 NM, 443.9 D43 (465)
373 SDLLW, p.111
374 JFLT, p.35 (D2.135)
375 LBS, 3, p.433
376 BL, p.277
377 GPC, p.557
378 MM, p.71
379 St. P. + M. p.57 (D5O1, 559)
380 HM, 4, p.136

381 HM, 4, p.131
382 St. P + M, p.93 (D5O1, 413)
383 NM, 260, (3520)
384 Arch. Camb., 1933, pp.310, 311
385 HM, 4, p.157
386 HM, 4, p.154
387 EWM, p.185
388 BL, p.244
389 BL, p.216, EWM, p.180
390 NM, 422.5 (2443)
391 Arch. Camb., 1895, p.32
392 BL, p.394
393 BL, p.187, EWM, p.175
394 ETD, p.24
395 BDD, 1, p.32
396 BDD, 1, p.81
397 BDD, 1, p.189
398 NM, 423.3 (4966)
399 LBS, 4, p.296
400 BL, p.123, EWM, p.167
401 BL, p.123
402 PNT p.280
403 BL, p.122, EWM, p.166
404 NM, 417, 1 (2383)
405 CPNE, p.125
406 LEA, p.25
407 LEA, p.55
408 LEA, p.79
409 NM, 453.7 D43 (3860)
410 NM, 453.7 D43 (3906)
411 NM, 260 (4578)
412 NM 453.7 (4374)
413 BL, p.211
414 IW, 6, pp.10,110
415 HM, 4, p.185
416 HM, 4, p.9
417 TPM, 77-86, p.1581
418 LBS, 3, p.392
419 BL, pp.171, 172
420 JFLT, p.41 (D583.6)
421 HM, 1, p.293
422 NM, 417.3 (5163)
423 LBS, 3, p.390
424 BL, p.228, EWM, p.182
425 CAPRW, p.267 (7948)
426 NM, 416 (5159)
427 NM, 417.4 (2417)
428 LBS, 3, pp.248, 249
429 BL, p.241, EWM, p.184
430 NM, 417.5 (3968)
431 MM, p.81
432 GPC, p.562
433 HM, 2, p.232
434 ECPCW, p.237
435 HM, 1, p.327
436 BL, p.233, EWM, p.183
437 SCP, p.103
438 TPM, 77-86, p.1577
439 BL, p.282
440 NM, 423.6 (6792)
441 HM, 2, p.230
442 NM, 442 (5093)
443 NM, 449 (5195)
444 SDLLW, p.119
445 NM, 416 (2289)
446 GPC, p.1251
447 GPC, p.2172
448 ETD, p.22
449 PNDP, pp.40, 41
450 CPNE, p.168
451 ECPCW, p.290
452 CAPRW, p.118 (4101)
453 CAPRW, p.102 (3360)
454 SCP, p.9
455 NM, 435.6 (3742)
456 EWM, p.177
457 LBS, 4, pp.353-362
458 EARWD, 2, p.719
459 NM, 428 (3976)
460 NM, 428 (5685)

461 'A Guide to Roman Remains in Britain', R.J.A. Wilson, 1985, p.82
462 MB, p.123; HM, 4, p.302
463 K.T. p.22 (D337 11/1)
464 K.T. p.17 (D337 5/1)
465 K.T. p.21 (D337 5/13)
466 K.T. p.15 (D337 9/10)
467 BL, p.235. EWM, p.183
468 PNT p.28I
469 BL, p.292, EWM, p.328
470 NM, 421.3 (2430)
471 HM, 4, p.50
472 DP, 2, p.290
473 HM, 4, p.252
474 NM, 431.3 (5711)
475 NM, 431.3 (5220)
476 SWMRS, 2, p.198
477 HM, 2, p.162
478 PNG, 3, p.234
479 PNRB, p.284
480 BL, p.186, EWM, p.175
481 BL, p.175
482 BL, p.276
483 DB, 1, p.180
484 LEA, p.87
485 EARWD, 2, p.748
486 NM, 140 (5235)
487 NM, 140 (5040)
488 NTCB, p.137
489 BL, p.191, EWM, p.176
490 BL,p.179, EWM, p.173
491 NM, 424.3 (4540)
492 NM, 424.3 (4491)
493 NCPNW p.99
494 HM, 4, p.52
495 NT p.322
496 NM, 424 (5386)
497 NCPNW, p.251
498 HM, 4, p.273
499 PNH, p.160
500 BDD, 1, p.128
501 HM, 4, p.23
502 HM, 4, p.9
503 NCPNW, p.263
504 MD, 1, p.52
505 BDD, 1, p.8
506 BDD, 1, p.51
507 BDD, 1, p.117
508 HM, 2. p.196
509 PNT p.282
510 HM, 4, p.214
511 CAM,1, p.81
512 BL, p.328
513 HM, 4, p.7
514 SCP, p.113
515 Med Mon., p.22
516 BL, p.284
517 SWMRS, 2, p.74
518 SWMRS, 2, p.193
519 NM, 412.6 (5110)
520 NM, 434.4 (4094)
521 BL, p.218, EWM, p.180
522 BL, p.221
523 CChR, 3pp.96, 97
524 HM, 2, pp.256, 257
525 BDD, 2, p.375
526 BDD, 2, p.413
527 BDD, 2, p.464
528 LBS, 3, p.459
529 CPNE, p.183
530 BMR, 2, p.218
531 NM, 428 (5692)
532 NCPNW, p.256
533 BL, p.150, EWM, p.169
534 HM, 2, p.257
535 ECPCW, p.229
536 HM, 4, p.45
537 NM, 431.3 (2549)
538 NM, 140 (5212)

539 PNG, 3, p.124
540 BPNHS, p.300
541 ECPCW, p.225
542 EARWD, 2, p.670
543 BL, p.323
544 NM, 425.3 (5663)
545 NM, 425.3 (237)
546 MA, p.388-9
547 'Lexicon Cornu-Brittanicum', Rev. R. Williams, 1839, p.62
548 GPC, p.528
549 BL, p.262
550 HM, 4, p.97
551 BL, p.142
552 BL, p.143
553 BL, p.166
554 HM, 4, p.6
555 NM, 417.7 (4025)
556 CAPRW, p.149
557 HM, 4, p.53
558 BL, p.369
559 BL, p.173
560 HM, 4, p.50
561 NU, p.102
562 NTCB, p.159
563 HM, 2, p.1
564 NCPNW, pp.252,253
565 HM, 4, p.236
566 HM, 4, p.243
567 ODPN, p.384
568 BL, p.241, EWM, p.184
569 BL, p.246, EWM, p.185
570 NCPNW, p.263
571 BL, p.284
572 NCPNW, p.255
573 HM, 4, p.41
574 PNWG, p.49
575 BMR, 2, p.218
576 NCPNW, p.254
577 HM, 4, p.11
578 HM, 4, p.267
579 ETD, p.31
580 ODPN, p.391
581 CPNE, p.140
582 BL, p.291
583 HM, 4, p,93
584 NCPNW, p.249
585 HM, 4, p.80
586 DP, 4, p.371
587 EARWD, 2, p.609
588 BL, p.219
589 NM, 453 (558)
590 PNF, p.98
591 BDD, 1, p.40
592 LBS, 1, p.174
593 BL, p.235
594 EARWD, 2, p.715
595 CARWM, p.459
596 LBS, 1, p.264
597 BL, p.165. EWM, p.171
598 BL, p.158
599 BDD, 2, p.367
600 LBS, 2, p.242
601 BL, pp.171, 172 EWM, p.172
602 BL, p.74, EWM, p.166
603 BL, p.265
604 BL, p.272
605 LBS, 3, p.433
606 BL, p.225
607 Mon, 7, p.1022
608 BDD, 2, p.333
609 HM, 4, p.287
610 HM, 4, p.295
611 LBS, 1, p.101
612 BL, p.291
613 HM, 4, p.74
614 BDD, 1, p.111
615 EARWD, 2, p.662
616 SCP, p.9
617 CAPRW, p.390

618 BL, p.329
619 NM, 421.3 (5564)
620 BT, p.202
621 CIPM, 1, p.8
622 CARWM, p.137
623 DP, 3, p.182
624 NCPNW, p.268
625 HM, 1, p.222
626 PNG, 3, p.247
627 ODPN, p.438
628 HM, 4, p.103
629 NCPNW, p.252
630 HM, 4, p.103
631 BL, p.141
632 BL, p.282
633 AC, p.39
634 EARWD, 2, p.751
635 BL, p.209, EWM, p.179
636 BL, p.156
637 BL, p.200, EWM, p.177
638 BL, p.199
639 BL, p.217
640 NM, 441 (5078)
641 NM, 441 (5182)
642 HM, 2, p.129
643 BL, p.370
644 BL, pp.196, 374
645 BL, p.217, EWM, p.186
646 BL, p.218
647 SBMR, 2, p.241
648 Arch. Camb., 1855, p.122
649 PNWG, p.59
650 HM, 2, p.98
651 CAPRW, p.358
652 VSBG, p.154
653 BDD, 1, p.112
654 NM, 442 (4994)
655 EARWD, 2, p.662
656 FPN, p.169-170
657 PNRB, p.285
658 BL, p.210, EWM, p.179
659 VSBG, p.134
660 EARWD, 2, p.637
661 Gir., 6, p.47
662 HM, 3, p.226
663 PM, 147, 953
664 NU, p.71
665 PNRB, p.328
666 PNWG, p.61
667 BL, p.250, EWM, p.185
668 NM, 428 (5681)
669 W, p.15
670 LBS, 4, p.239
671 BL, p.li (Introduction)
672 GPC, p.1772
673 HM, 4, p.280
674 HM, 4, p.191
675 CEEP, p.40
676 NM, 423.2 (2453)
677 HM, 4, p.223
678 BL, p.241, EWM, p.184
679 EARWD, 2, p.615
680 BDD, 1, p.29
681 BDD, 1, p.220
682 BL, p.201, EWM, p.177
683 BL, p.375
684 BDD, 1, p.24
685 DB, 1, p.162
686 APDBIW, p.369
687 NM, 449, (5103)
688 DL, p.407
689 HM, 4, p.161
690 HM. 1, p.126
691 EANC, p.137
692 PNDP, p.201
693 CPE, p.134
694 HM, 4, p.275
695 HM, 4, p.229
696 CPR, p.164
697 CIPM, 1, p.222

698 BL, p.179
699 BMR, 3, p.231 (2239)
700 BDD.1,107 (1261)
701 CARWM, p.138
702 BDD, 1, p.20
703 BL, p.242
704 NM, 436, D43 (5809)
705 CChR, 3, p.98
706 HM, 4, p.147
707 BMR, 2, p.218 (1787)
708 HM, 4, p.228
709 BL, p.154, WCD, p.313
710 WCD, p.362
711 WCD, p.80
712 NU, p.10
713 FPN, p.161
714 Ellis D. M.,
M. A. Thesis, U. C. Aberystwyth,
(1935), Pts. I and II, p.440